Parties

Parties

Bloomsbury Books
London

This edition published 1995 by Bloomsbury Books,
an imprint of The Godfrey Cave Group,
42 Bloomsbury Street, London, WC1B 3QJ.

ISBN 1 85471 582 8

Printed and bound in Great Britain

Contents

Miniature Savoury Choux Puffs 7

Herb Pretzels 8

Savoury Nibbles 9

Sesame Crackers 10

Garlicky Smoked Roe Dip 11

Dates Stuffed with Bresaola and Mozzarella 12

Caviare Canapés 13

Prunes Stuffed with Wild Rice and Turkey 14

Herring Roe Canapés 15

Smoked Salmon Roll-Ups 16

Sushi of Prawn and Seaweed
  Wrapped in Radicchio 17

Stuffed Squid Rings 18

Minced Lamb and Burghul 19

Pork Sticks with Tomato and Fennel Sauce 20

Fiery Chick-Peas 21

Courgette Soufflés 22

Fir Apple Potato Canapés 23

Baby Potatoes Coated with Herbs and Parmesan 24

Anchovy-Tomato Dip 25

Aubergine, Tomato and Crab Croustades 26

Mussels on the Half Shell 27

Red-Hot Monkfish 28

Two-Salmon Wontons 29

Sesame-Prawn Toasts 30

Bacon and Monkfish Rolls 31

Halibut Kievski 32

Turkey Twists 33

Pork Phyllo Pastries 34

Bacon and Date Pinwheels 35

Ox Heart Brochettes 36

Salmon and Watercress Rolls 37

Vegetable Purées in Chicory 38
Spinach and Salmon Canapés 39
Pineapple Chunks Wrapped in Spicy Beef 40
Garlic Pâté 41
Mushroom and Chestnut Pâté with Madeira 42
Chocolate and Ginger Cheesecakes 43
Chocolate-Dipped Stuffed Prunes 44
Chocolate Rum Cups 45
Chocolate Brandy Snaps 46
Pecan-Chestnut Sweetmeats 47
Maple Sweetmeats 48
Glazed Fruits... 49
Fruited Turkish Coffee Squares 50
Fig and Orange Petits Fours 51
Cherry-Chocolate Meringue Nests 52
Cocktail Croutons 53
Oatmeal Cheese Straws 54
Labne Cocktail Balls 55
Stuffed Cherry Tomatoes 56
Lemon and Tarragon Scallop Croustades 57
Herb Popcorn.. 58
Plantain Crisps 59
Aubergine Sausages... 60
Goujons with Dill and Gherkin Dip 61
Stuffed Pasta Rings 62
Sausage Rolls 63
Pink Trout Mousse 64
Artichoke Stuffed Mushrooms 65
Pasta, Corn and Leek Salad 66
Feta and Phyllo Parcels 67
Mange-Tout with Purée 68
Sigara Borek with Asparagus and Parmesan 69
Veal with Apricot and Nut Stuffing 70
Liver and Fruit Pâté 71

Miniature Savoury Choux Puffs

Makes about 35 puffs

Working time: about 40 minutes

Total time: about 1 hour

Per 5 puffs:

Calories 65

Protein 1g

Cholesterol 25mg

Total fat 4g

Saturated fat 2g

Sodium 65mg

125 g	plain flour	**4 oz**
¼ tsp	salt	**¼ tsp**
2	eggs	**2**
1	egg white	**1**
90 g	polyunsaturated margarine	**3 oz**

60 g	Parmesan cheese, finely grated	**2 oz**
1	garlic clove, crushed	**1**
2 tbsp	finely cut fresh chives	**2 tbsp**
1 tbsp	mixed dried herbs	**1 tbsp**

Preheat the oven to 220°C (425°F or Mark 7). Line several baking sheets with non-stick baking parchment. Have ready three piping bags, each fitted with a 1 cm (½ inch) plain nozzle. Sift the flour and salt. Lightly beat the eggs and the egg white together.

Put the margarine into a saucepan with ¼ litre (8 fl oz) of cold water and heat gently until the margarine melts, then bring to the boil. Remove the pan from the heat and tip in the flour, stirring quickly with a wooden spoon. Return the pan to a moderate heat and stir for a few seconds until the mixture forms a ball. Remove from the heat.

Very gradually add the eggs to the flour and water paste, beating vigorously between each addition with a wooden spoon or a hand-held electric mixer.

Beat the Parmesan and garlic into the choux paste. Put one third of the mixture into a piping bag. Put another third of the mixture into a small bowl and beat in the chives, then spoon into another piping bag. Beat the mixed herbs into the remaining choux paste and spoon into the third piping bag.

Pipe the choux mixtures on to the lined baking sheets in small mounds about 1 cm (½ inch) in diameter, spaced apart. Bake in the oven until well risen, golden-brown and crisp—20 to 25 minutes. Remove from the baking sheets immediately and let cool. Serve the puffs within a couple of hours.

Herb Pretzels

Makes about
40 pretzels

Working time:
about 45
minutes

Total time:
about 1 hour

Per 5 pretzels:
Calories
185
Protein
5g
Cholesterol
35mg
Total fat
11g
Saturated fat
3g
Sodium
205mg

125 g	plain flour	**4 oz**	**1 tsp**	mixed dried herbs	**1 tsp**
60 g	wholemeal flour	**2 oz**	**90 g**	polyunsaturated margarine	**3 oz**
¼ tsp	salt	**¼ tsp**	**1**	small egg, beaten	**1**
½ tsp	baking powder	**½ tsp**	**30 g**	Parmesan cheese, finely grated	**1 oz**

Preheat the oven to 200°C (400°F or Mark 6). Grease several baking sheets.

Sift the flours, salt and baking powder into a mixing bowl, adding any bran left in the sieve. Mix in the herbs, then rub in the margarine until the mixture resembles fine breadcrumbs. Make a well in the centre of the flour. Pour 5 tablespoons of boiling water into the well, then mix with a round-bladed knife to form a soft dough. Knead the dough on a very lightly floured surface to smooth.

Divide the dough into about 40 small pieces. Take one piece of dough and roll it out with your hands into a thin strand, about 30 cm (12 inches) long.

Form a pretzel by shaping the strand into a curve, with its ends towards you. Cross the ends over, then take their points up to the centre of the curve and press them firmly in position. Place the pretzel on a baking sheet. Shape the remaining pieces of dough in the same way.

Brush the pretzels lightly with the beaten egg, then sprinkle with the Parmesan. Bake in the oven for about 15 minutes, until lightly browned. Carefully remove the pretzels to a wire rack to cool.

Savoury Nibbles

Makes about 250

Working time: about 30 minutes

Total time: about 40 minutes

Per 5 nibbles:
Calories 85
Protein 2g
Cholesterol 20mg
Total fat 6g
Saturated fat 2g
Sodium 120mg

175 g	plain flour	**6 oz**
½ tsp	salt	**½ tsp**
½ tsp	baking powder	**½ tsp**
90 g	polyunsaturated margarine	**3 oz**
90 g	Cheddar cheese, finely grated	**3 oz**

1	egg, lightly beaten	**1**
1 tsp	curry powder	**1 tsp**
1	garlic clove	**1**
2 tbsp	finely chopped parsley	**2 tbsp**

Preheat the oven to 200°C (400°F or Mark 6). Grease several baking sheets.

Sift the flour, half of the salt and the baking powder into a mixing bowl. Rub the margarine into the flour until the mixture resembles fine breadcrumbs. Mix in the cheese. Add the egg and mix together with a round-bladed knife to form a soft dough.

Gently knead the dough on a lightly floured surface until smooth, then roll out to an oblong approximately 45 by 30 cm (18 by 12 inches). Using a fluted pastry wheel, cut the dough into long, thin strips, about 2 cm (¾ inch) wide. Cut across the strips to make diamond shapes, oblongs or squares. Place the tiny biscuits on the baking sheets and bake in the oven until they are golden-brown—8 to 10 minutes. Remove the biscuits to wire racks to cool. Immediately, sift the curry powder over half of the biscuits.

Put the garlic into a small mortar with the remaining salt and crush with a pestle until creamy. Mix in the parsley. When the plain biscuits are cool, put them into a large bowl, add the garlic mixture and mix very gently until the biscuits are evenly coated. Serve the biscuits in separate bowls.

Sesame Crackers

Makes about 100 crackers

Working time: about 30 minutes

Total time: about 55 minutes

Per 5 crackers:
Calories
95
Protein
3g
Cholesterol
20mg
Total fat
5g
Saturated fat
3g
Sodium
70mg

250 g	plain flour	**8 oz**	
¼tsp	salt	**¼ tsp**	
¾tsp	baking powder	**¾ tsp**	
60 g	unsalted butter	**2 oz**	

90 g	Cheddar cheese, finely grated	**3 oz**	
1	small egg, beaten	**1**	
30 g	sesame seeds	**1 oz**	

Preheat the oven to 200°C (400°F or Mark 6). Grease several baking sheets.

Sift the flour, salt and baking powder into a mixing bowl. Rub the butter into the flour until the mixture resembles fine breadcrumbs. Mix in the cheese, then make a well in the centre of the flour. Pour 5 tablespoons of water into the well and mix with a round-bladed knife to make a soft dough. Knead the dough on a lightly floured surface to smooth.

Roll the dough out very thinly, then prick well all over with a fork. Using a 3 cm (1¼ inch) plain round cutter, cut out rounds and place them on the baking sheets. Re-knead and re-roll the trimmings, then cut out more rounds. Continue until the dough is used up.

Brush the crackers with the beaten egg, then sprinkle with the sesame seeds Bake in the oven until golden-brown and crisp—20 to 25 minutes. Place the crackers on wire racks to cool.

Garlicky Smoked Roe Dip

Serves 6

Working time: about 15 minutes

Total time: about 20 minutes

Calories 80

Protein 6g

Cholesterol 0mg

Total fat 3g

Saturated fat trace

Sodium 120mg

90 g	white bread, crusts removed	**3 oz**	**1**	small garlic clove, crushed	**1**
90 g	smoked cod's roe, skinned	**3 oz**		freshly ground black pepper	
60 g	medium-fat curd cheese	**2 oz**		lemon wedges, for garnish	
$\frac{1}{2}$	lemon, juice only	$\frac{1}{2}$			

Place the bread in a small bowl, cover with water and leave to soak for a few minutes.

Remove the bread from the water and squeeze it thoroughly dry, then place it in a food processor with the cod's roe, curd cheese, lemon juice, crushed garlic and some freshly ground black pepper. Process until the mixture is smooth.

Turn the purée into a small bowl and serve it garnished with the lemon wedges.

Dates Stuffed with Bresaola and Mozzarella

Makes 30
stuffed dates

Working (and
total) time:
about 15
minutes

Per stuffed
date:
Calories
20
Protein
1g
Cholesterol
1mg
Total fat
2g
Saturated fat
1g
Sodium
40mg

1 tbsp	virgin olive oil	**1 tbsp**
	freshly ground black pepper	
125 g	mozzarella, cut into 30 sticks,	**4 oz**
	5 by 1 by 1 cm (2 by ½ by ½ inch)	

15	fresh dates, halved, stones removed	**15**
30 g	bresaola, cut into 1 cm (½ inch)	**1 oz**
	wide ribbons	
	fresh parsley sprigs, for garnish	

Pour the olive oil into a shallow dish, grind in some black pepper and add the mozzarella; carefully turn the cheese sticks in the oil to coat them thoroughly. Arrange the date halves, cut sides up, on a serving platter.

Wind the ribbons of bresaola diagonally round the sticks of mozzarella, and lay them on the date halves. Serve garnished with the sprigs of parsley.

Caviare Canapés

Makes 18
canapés

Working (and
total) time:
about 15
minutes

Per canapé:
Calories
20
Protein
1g
Cholesterol
10mg
Total fat
1g
Saturated fat
trace
Sodium
55mg

| 3 | slices dark pumpernickel | 3 | 20 g | black caviare or lumpfish roe | ¾ oz |
| 150 g | fromage frais | 5 oz | 20 g | red caviare or lumpfish roe | ¾ oz |

Cut each slice of pumpernickel in half lengthwise, then cut each half into three to make six pieces about 4 cm (1 ½ inches) square. Arrange the pumpernickel squares on a serving dish or plate.

Spread a little of the *fromage frais* on to the centre of each piece of pumpernickel, leaving the edges of the bread showing. Spoon about ¼ teaspoon of black roe on to half the bread squares, then spoon a smaller amount of red roe on to the middle of the black roe. Spoon the red roe on to the remaining bread squares, with a smaller amount of black roe on top. Serve the canapés immediately.

Prunes Stuffed with Wild Rice and Turkey

Makes 14
stuffed prunes

Working time:
about 30
minutes

Total time:
about 1 hour
and 30
minutes

Per stuffed
prune:
Calories
25
Protein
2g
Cholesterol
5mg
Total fat
trace
Saturated fat
trace
Sodium
30mg

30 g	wild rice	**1 oz**	**60 g**	smoked turkey or chicken,		**2 oz**
¼ litre	unsalted chicken, beef	**8 fl oz**		finely chopped		
	or veal stock or water			freshly grated nutmeg		
14	large ready-to-eat prunes	**14**	**¼ tsp**	salt		**¼ tsp**
1 tbsp	finely cut chives	**1 tbsp**		freshly ground black pepper		

Put the rice and stock or water into a heavy-bottom saucepan, bring to the boil, then simmer, covered, until the husks of the rice have split—50 to 60 minutes. Drain off any remaining cooking liquid and set the rice aside to cool.

Using a sharp knife, slit open one side of each prune from end to end. Mix the turkey with the rice, season with some nutmeg, the salt and a little pepper and stuff the prunes with this mixture. Sprinkle chives over the stuffed prunes and serve.

Editor's Note: The prunes used in this recipe are sold for eating straight from the packet, and do not require either soaking or stoning. If you use ordinary dried prunes, soak them for 10 minutes in boiling water with a dash of Madeira, and then stone them.

Herring Roe Canapés

Makes 24 canapés

Working (and total) time: about 25 minutes

Per canapé:

Calories
20

Protein
1g

Cholesterol
30mg

Total fat
1g

Saturated fat
0g

Sodium
35mg

250 g	soft herring roe	**8 oz**
1 tsp	grapeseed oil	**1 tsp**
½ tsp	Dijon mustard	**½ tsp**
1 tbsp	crème fraîche	**1 tbsp**
⅛ tsp	cayenne pepper	**⅛ tsp**
½ tsp	fresh lemon juice	**½ tsp**

2 tsp	finely cut chives, plus a few chives for garnish	**2 tsp**
1	small loaf dark rye bread, cut into thin slices	**1**
24	small capers, rinsed and drained	**24**

Rinse the roe and cut away any dark blood vessels with a pair of scissors. Gently wipe the roe clean.

Heat the grapeseed oil in a heavy frying pan over medium heat, and fry the roe gently with the mustard for 4 to 5 minutes; break up the roe with a spoon while it is cooking. Place the cooked roe in a fine-meshed nylon sieve, drain off any remaining liquid, then press the roe through the sieve into a bowl. Mix the *crème fraîche*, lemon juice, finely cut chives and cayenne pepper into the roe.

Using a 4 cm (1½ inch) round fluted pastry cutter, cut out 24 rounds from the rye bread. Spread the roe mixture on the bread circles, and garnish with the capers and chives. Arrange the canapés on a serving plate.

Smoked Salmon Roll-Ups

Makes 16 roll-ups

Working (and total) time: about 30 minutes

Per roll-up:

Calories
30

Protein
3g

Cholesterol
5mg

Total fat
1g

Saturated fat
trace

Sodium
180mg

16	baby sweetcorn	**16**
15 g	dill, finely chopped	**½ oz**
	freshly ground black pepper	
60 g	fromage frais	**2 oz**

125 g	smoked salmon, cut into 16 thin strips	**4 oz**
16	chives or slivers of spring onion	**16**
	lime wedges, for garnish	

Pour enough water into a saucepan to fill it about 2.5 cm (1 inch) deep. Set a vegetable steamer in the pan and bring the water to the boil. Put the sweetcorn in the steamer and steam until just soft—about 5 minutes. Remove from the steamer and allow to cool.

Blend the dill and some freshly ground black pepper into the *fromage frais*, and spread each strip of smoked salmon with a little of this mixture. Roll a strip of salmon round each baby sweetcorn, and tie a chive or spring onion sliver round the salmon. Arrange on a serving dish and garnish with the lime wedges.

Editor's Note: Smoked salmon trout may be substituted for the smoked salmon in this recipe.

Sushi of Prawn and Seaweed Wrapped in Radicchio

Makes 24 sushi

Working time: about 30 minutes

Total time about 1 hour and 20 minutes

Calories
40

Protein
1g

Cholesterol
5mg

Total fat
trace

Saturated fat
trace

Sodium
75mg

200 g	sushi rice	**7 oz**
1 tsp	salt	**1 tsp**
2 tsp	sugar	**2 tsp**
24	chives, or two spring onions cut into very fine ribbons	**24**

90 g	shelled cooked prawns	**3 oz**
⅛ tsp	wasabi powder	**⅛ tsp**
1½ tsp	dried wakame	**1½ tsp**
12	large radicchio leaves	**12**
2 tbsp	rice vinegar, plus 1 tsp	**2 tbsp**

Rinse the rice three times in five times its volume of water, then leave it in a sieve for about 45 minutes to absorb any residual water.

Put the rice in a saucepan with ¼ litre (8 fl oz) of water and bring to the boil, partially covered, over high heat. Reduce the heat, cover and simmer for 10 minutes. Leave the pan on the stove, with the heat turned off, for 10 to 15 minutes. Dissolve the salt and sugar in 2 tablespoons of the vinegar, and mix into the rice with a wet wooden spoon.

While the rice is cooking, blanch the chives or spring onions by pouring boiling water over them in a deep bowl. Refresh immediately in cold water, drain, then dry on paper towels to dry. Devein and dice the prawns. Mix the wasabi powder with a little water to make a paste. Soak the wakame in water for 5 to 10 minutes (it will quadruple in size), then squeeze it dry in a tea towel.

Cut each radicchio leaf in half lengthwise and trim away the centre ribs. Mix the remaining vinegar with 3 tablespoons of water; dip your fingers in this and spread the rice over three quarters of the length of each leaf, pressing it down. Spread a thin layer of wasabi paste over the rice, followed by the wakame, and then the prawns.

Roll up each leaf to enclose the rice and filling. Tie a ribbon of chive or spring onion round each sushi, and trim the sides.

Stuffed Squid Rings

Makes
32 rings

Working
time: about
30 minutes

Total time:
about 1 hour
15 minutes

Per ring:
Calories
15
Protein
3g
Cholesterol
35mg
Total fat
trace
Saturated fat
trace
Sodium
25mg

8	small young squid (about 500 g/1 lb), cleaned and skinned	8
8	leaves red lollo or other crisp lettuce, washed and dried	8
100 g	turbot or halibut, skinned and diced	3 oz
2 tbsp	low-sodium soy sauce or shoyu	2 tbsp
30 cl	unsalted fish or vegetable stock	½ pint
2.5 cm	piece fresh ginger root, finely sliced	1 inch
1 tbsp	molasses	1 tbsp
1 tbsp	balsamic vinegar, or ½ tbsp red wine vinegar	1 tbsp

Drain and dry the squid tentacles and pouches with paper towels. Spread open a lettuce leaf and trim it to the same length as one of the pouches. Place a set of tentacles along the centre line of the leaf and arrange an eighth of the diced fish on the leaf at the tentacle tips. Roll up the leaf tightly and place the lettuce package inside one of the pouches. Trim away any excess leaf and secure the pouch opening with a cocktail stick. Stuff the remaining pouches in the same way.

Combine the stock, soy sauce, ginger, molasses and vinegar in a saucepan or fireproof casserole, and bring to the boil. Add the stuffed squid, cover and simmer gently until the squid are tender—30 to 45 minutes. As both the squid and the lettuce will shrink considerably, releasing juices as they cook, turning should not be necessary, but check occasionally that all surfaces are covered by liquid and add more water if they are not. Allow the squid to cool in their liquid, then chill in the refrigerator.

Shortly before serving, drain the squid and remove the cocktail sticks. Slice each pouch into four rings.

Minced Lamb and Burghul

Makes about 30 discs

Working (and total) time: about 20 minutes

Per 3 discs:
Calories 175
Protein 18g
Cholesterol 35mg
Total fat 5g
Saturated fat 2g
Sodium 150mg

500 g	lean lamb for mincing, trimmed of all fat	1 lb
250 g	fine-grade burghul	8 oz
1	large onion, grated	1
1 tsp	ground cumin	1 tsp
1½ tsp	cayenne pepper	1½ tsp
1 tsp	salt	1 tsp
	freshly ground black pepper	
4	spring onions, finely chopped	4
2 tbsp	finely chopped parsley	2 tbsp
	small leaves of crisp lettuce	

Pass the meat three times through the fine blade of a mincer. Put the burghul in a large bowl, pour boiling water over it and leave it to stand for 2 minutes. Drain the burghul in a sieve and rinse it under cold running water; scoop up handfuls and squeeze out excess water, returning the squeezed-out burghul to the bowl as you proceed.

Combine the minced meat, grated onion, cumin and cayenne pepper in a food processor to make a coarse paste. Tip the paste into the bowl of burghul, add the salt and some freshly ground black pepper, and knead for at least 10 minutes to mix all the ingredients thoroughly; add about 2 tablespoons of cold water while kneading to moisten the mixture.

When the paste is smooth, mix in the finely chopped spring onions and the parsley. Make about 30 little balls, then flatten these with your thumb into small discs. Serve the discs on individual lettuce leaves for eating with the fingers.

Pork Sticks with Tomato and Fennel Sauce

Makes about 40 sticks

Working time: about 30 minutes

Total time about 1 hour and 20 minutes

Per stick:

Calories 30

Protein 2g

Cholesterol 30mg

Total fat 2g

Saturated fat 1g

Sodium 30mg

400 g	pork fillet in one piece	**14 oz**
2 tsp	virgin olive oil	**2 tsp**
½ tsp	fennel seeds, lightly crushed	**½ tsp**
¼ tsp	salt	**¼ tsp**
	freshly ground black pepper	
350 g	bulb fennel, feathery tops chopped, bulbs halved	**12 oz**
1	thick lemon slice	**1**
	Tomato and fennel sauce	
2 tbsp	virgin olive oil	**2 tbsp**

1	garlic clove, finely chopped	**1**
250 g	bulb fennel trimmed, chopped	**8 oz**
½ tsp	fennel seeds, lightly crushed	**½ tsp**
½	orange, pared rind only	**½**
4 tbsp	anise-flavoured spirit	**4 tbsp**
500 g	tomatoes, skinned, seeded, chopped	**1 lb**
¼ tsp	salt	**¼ tsp**
	freshly ground black pepper	
	pared orange rind, julienned, for garnish	

Preheat the oven to 230°C (450°F or Mark 8). Brush the pork with the oil and rub with the fennel seeds. Roast the pork for 20 to 25 minutes, then season with the salt and a little pepper, wrap loosely in foil and leave to cool.

Meanwhile, make the sauce. Heat the oil in a sauté pan and cook the garlic gently for a minute or two. Stir in the chopped fennel, crushed fennel seeds, orange rind, anise-flavoured spirit and some pepper. Cover and simmer for 10 minutes. Add the tomatoes and simmer for a further 10 minutes; allow to

cool. Discard the orange rind, then purée the sauce. Add the salt and set aside.

Parboil the fennel bulbs with the lemon slice for about 5 minutes, or until the fennel is just tender. Drain, and discard the lemon; refresh the fennel under cold water and drain well. Cut into forty 1 cm (½ inch) cubes.

Unwrap the fillet and cut into 2 cm (¾ inch) cubes. Thread cocktail sticks with one piece of fennel and one of pork. Dip in the chopped fennel tops and arrange on a dish. Garnish the sauce with the julienned orange rind.

Fiery Chick-Peas

Serves 14

Working time:
about 20
minutes

Total time:
about 2 hours
and
30 minutes
(includes
soaking)

Calories
175

Protein
7g

Cholesterol
0mg

Total fat
9g

Saturated fat
1g

Sodium
40mg

500 g	dried chick-peas	1 lb	1 tsp	cayenne pepper	1 tsp
6 tbsp	virgin olive oil	6 tbsp	¼ tsp	salt	¼ tsp
1	garlic clove	1			

Rinse the chick-peas under cold running water. Put them in a large, heavy-bottomed saucepan and pour in enough cold water to cover them by about 5 cm (2 inches). Discard any chick-peas that float to the surface. Cover the pan, leaving the lid ajar, and bring the water to the boil; cook the chick-peas for 2 minutes. Turn off the heat, cover the pan, and leave to soak for at least 1 hour. (Alternatively, soak the chick-peas overnight in cold water.)

When the chick-peas finish soaking, drain them well in a colander. Return them to the pan and pour in enough water to cover them by about 5 cm (2 inches). Bring the liquid to a simmer, and cook over medium-low heat until quite tender—45 minutes to 1 hour. (If they appear to be drying out at any point,

pour in more water.) When cooked, drain and allow to cool.

Dry the chick-peas thoroughly on paper towels or a clean tea towel. Heat the oil in a heavy frying pan until shimmering. Toss in the chick-peas, stir around for a few seconds, then add the garlic.

Reduce the heat and sauté the chickpeas, stirring and tossing from time to time, until their skins are golden-brown—20 to 25 minutes. If the chick-peas pop and jump, either reduce the heat or cover the pan.

Tip the chick-peas on to multiple thicknesses of paper towels and roll them around to remove as much oil as possible. While hot, put them in a bowl, add the cayenne pepper and salt, and toss well. Serve warm, to be eaten with the fingers.

Courgette Soufflés

5	courgettes, each about 18 cm (7 inches) long, ends trimmed	5
1 tsp	polyunsaturated margarine	**1 tsp**
15 g	plain flour	**½ oz**
4 tbsp	skimmed milk	**4 tbsp**
1	egg yolk	**1**

30 g	mature Cheddar cheese, grated	**1 oz**
¼ tsp	Dijon mustard	**¼ tsp**
¼ tsp	salt	**¼ tsp**
	freshly ground black pepper	
2	egg whites	**2**

Cut away thin, evenly spaced strips of skin from the length of each courgette to form a crimped effect. Cut each courgette into eight slices about 2 cm (¾ inch) thick. Using a small spoon, scoop out the centre of each slice, taking care not to pierce the base.

Preheat the oven to 220°C (425°F or Mark 7). Cook the courgettes in boiling water until bright green and almost tender—about 1 minute. Drain well, and arrange on a baking sheet lined with non-stick parchment paper.

For the filling, place the margarine, flour and milk in a small saucepan, and whisk until the ingredients are well blended. Place the pan over medium heat and bring to the boil,

whisking. Reduce the heat and cook gently for 5 minutes, still whisking. Remove from the heat and whisk in the egg yolk, cheese, mustard, seasoning, until evenly mixed.

In a clean bowl, whisk the egg whites until they are stiff but not dry. Add the egg white to the cheese sauce, one third at a time, carefully folding it into the mixture until all the egg white has been incorporated. Place teaspoons of the soufflé mixture into the courgette containers, filling each to the top.

Bake the soufflés at the top of the oven until the mixture has risen well and is golden-brown—5 to 8 minutes. Arrange the soufflés on a serving plate, and serve hot or warm.

Fir Apple Potato Canapés

Makes about
30 canapés

Working time:
about 20
minutes

Total time:
about 30
minutes

Per canapé:
Calories
25
Protein
1g
Cholesterol
5mg
Total fat
1g
Saturated fat
trace
Sodium
30mg

4	fir apple potatoes (350 g/12 oz), scrubbed and dried	4	4	orange segments, cut into slices, for garnish		4
30 g	unsalted butter	1 oz		**Celery topping**		
2	garlic cloves, crushed	2	2	sticks celery, finely chopped		2
1 tbsp	finely chopped celery leaves	1 tbsp	125 g	turkey breast fillet, chopped		4 oz
1 tbsp	finely chopped parsley	1 tbsp	1 tbsp	pine-nuts, chopped		1 tbsp
½ tsp	salt	½ tsp	1 tsp	finely grated orange rind		1 tsp
	freshly ground black pepper		1 tsp	Dijon mustard		1 tsp

Preheat the oven to 220°C (425°F or Mark 7). Cut the potatoes into 5 mm (¼ inch) slices and cook them in a saucepan of boiling water for 1 minute, until they are almost tender. Drain well and transfer to a bowl.

Put the butter, crushed garlic, chopped celery leaves, parsley, salt and a little pepper in the saucepan and stir until the butter has melted. Pour half of this on to the potato slices and toss well to coat them evenly.

Line a baking sheet with non-stick parchment paper. Remove the potatoes from the bowl with a slotted spoon, and space them out on the baking sheet. Bake in the oven until lightly browned—4 to 5 minutes.

While the potatoes are baking, prepare the topping. Add the chopped celery, turkey fillet, pine-nuts, orange rind and mustard to the remaining garlic butter in the saucepan. Cook over moderate heat for 1 minute, stirring occasionally. Add more pepper if desired.

Place spoonfuls of the mixture on top of each potato slice, dividing the mixture evenly. Return the potato slices to the top shelf of the oven and bake until the topping has set— about 5 minutes. Arrange the potato canapés on a serving plate and garnish each with a slice of orange. Serve hot or warm.

Baby Potatoes Coated with Herbs and Parmesan

1.5 kg	small new potatoes, scrubbed	**3 lb**
4 tbsp	virgin olive oil	**4 tbsp**
60 g	Parmesan cheese, freshly grated	**2 oz**
½ tsp	salt	**½ tsp**

30 g	fresh dill, chives, parsley or mint,	**1 oz**
	or any combination of these, chopped	
	freshly ground black pepper	

Boil the potatoes until they are just soft—about 15 minutes—then drain them thoroughly.

Place the oil, cheese, herbs and salt in a large bowl with a generous grinding of pepper. Add the potatoes and toss them until they are well coated with the mixture. Serve hot or warm, speared with cocktail sticks.

Anchovy-Tomato Dip

Serves 10

Working (and total) time: about 1 hour

Calories 55
Protein 3g
Cholesterol trace
Total fat 2g
Saturated fat trace
Sodium 155mg

7	garlic cloves	7
1 tbsp	virgin olive oil	1 tbsp
4	anchovy fillets, rinsed and drained	4
750 g	plum tomatoes, skinned, seeded and coarsely chopped	1½ lb
¾ tsp	powdered dried oregano	¾ tsp
1½ tbsp	tomato paste	1½ tbsp
1½ tbsp	red wine vinegar	1½ tbsp
1½ tsp	molasses or other dark brown sugar	1½ tsp

250 g	broccoli florets	8 oz
175 g	mushrooms	6 oz
1 tbsp	chopped fresh basil	1 tbsp
1	sweet red pepper, seeded, deribbed and cut into 2.5 cm (1 inch) squares	1
1	sweet yellow pepper, seeded, deribbed and cut into 2.5 cm (1 inch) squares	1
350 g	cauliflower florets	12 oz

Put the garlic and oil in a heavy saucepan and cook gently, crushing the garlic cloves as they soften. After about 10 minutes, add the anchovies and cook for a further 5 minutes, stirring and crushing the anchovies; do not allow the mixture to burn. Add the tomatoes, oregano, tomato paste, vinegar and sugar, and simmer for 20 to 30 minutes, stirring.

Meanwhile, pour enough water into a saucepan to fill it 2.5 cm (1 inch) deep. Set a steamer in the pan and bring the water to the boil. Put the broccoli in the steamer, cover tightly, and steam for just 1 minute. Remove from and set aside. Wipe the mushrooms, cut into bite-sized pieces and set aside.

Push the tomato sauce through a sieve over a bowl. Transfer the sauce to a small fondue pot and set over a gentle flame

Arrange the vegetables on a serving platter and provide fondue forks or long bamboo sticks for spearing the morsels and dipping them into the hot sauce.

Aubergine, Tomato and Crab Croustades

Makes 12 croustades

Working time: about 30 minutes

Total time: about 35 minutes

Per croustade:

Calories 90

Protein 4g

Cholesterol 10mg

Total fat 4g

Saturated fat 1g

Sodium 80mg

12	thin slices white bread	**12**
3 tbsp	virgin olive oil	**3 tbsp**
250 g	aubergine, peeled and roughly chopped	**8 oz**
125 g	tomatoes, skinned, seeded and roughly chopped	**4 oz**
½	lemon, juice only	**½**
½ tsp	salt	**½ tsp**
	freshly ground black pepper	
125 g	white crab meat, picked over	**4 oz**
	lemon slices, for garnish	
1	garlic clove finely chopped	**1**

Preheat the oven to 200°C (400°F or Mark 6).

Using a 7.5 cm (3 inch) diameter round pastry cutter, cut out a circle from each slice of bread, Brush both sides of the bread circles lightly with 2 tablespoons of the oil and press them firmly into 12 tartlet tins. Cook in the oven until the bread is golden-brown and has set into shape—about 10 minutes.

Meanwhile, prepare the filling. Heat the remaining oil in a heavy frying pan over medium heat and sauté the aubergine with the garlic. When the aubergine is well browned, stir in the tomato, lemon juice, salt and some pepper. Increase the heat to evaporate all the juices, then spoon the mixture into the croustade cases. Flake the crab meat and distribute it among the cases.

Cover the croustades loosely with aluminium foil or a sheet of greaseproof paper and return the tray to the hot oven for 5 minutes. Serve hot, garnished with the slices of lemon.

Mussels on the Half Shell

Makes 20
mussels

Working (and
total) time:
30 minutes

Per mussel:

Calories
25

Protein
4g

Cholesterol
10mg

Total fat
1g

Saturated fat
trace

Sodium
70mg

20	mussels (about 500g/1 lb) scrubbed and debearded	20
1	lemon, cut into wedges	1
	Tomato and fennel relish	
2 tsp	virgin olive oll	2 tsp
60 g	bulb fennel, finely chooped	2 oz
250 g	tomatoes, skinned, seeded and chopped	8 oz
$\frac{1}{2}$ tsp	sherry vinegar	$\frac{1}{2}$ tsp
1 tsp	tomato paste	1 tsp
1	garlic clove, crushed	1
1 tsp	salt	1 tsp
	freshly ground black pepper	
15 g	wild fennel or parsley, finely chopped	$\frac{1}{2}$ oz

Pour 4 tablespoons of water into a large pan. Add the mussels, cover the pan and bring the water to the boil. Steam the mussels until their shells open—4 to 5 minutes. Discard any mussels that remain closed.

Remove the top shell from each of the mussels and discard. Using your fingers or a spoon, sever the connective tissue that attaches the mussel to the bottom shell. Return the mussels to their half shells and place them in an ovenproof serving dish. Preheat the oven to 190°C (375°F or Mark 5).

To make the tomato and fennel relish, first pour the oil into a heavy-bottomed saucepan over medium heat and sauté the fennel until fairly soft—about 5 minutes. Add the tomatoes, vinegar, tomato paste, garlic, salt and some pepper, and simmer until the mixture is well reduced—about 10 minutes. Stir in the wild fennel or parsley.

Spoon a little of the relish on to each half mussel shell. Cover the dish with aluminium foil and put it in the oven for about 5 minutes, long enough for the mussels and relish to warm through. Serve immediately with the lemon wedges.

Red-Hot Monkfish

Makes about
50 bite-sized
pieces

Working time:
about 25
minutes

Total time:
about 1 hour
and 10
minutes

Per piece:

Calories
25

Protein
3g

Cholesterol
10mg

Total fat
1g

Saturated fat
trace

Sodium
20mg

1.25 kg	ripe tomatoes, roughly chopped, or 800 g/28 oz canned tomatoes, drained	**2½ lb**	**15 g**	fresh green chili pepper, seeded and finely chopped	**½ oz**
2½ tbsp	virgin olive oil	**2½ tbsp**	**⅛ tsp**	chili powder	**⅛ tsp**
1	small onion, finely chopped	**1**	**1 tsp**	caster sugar	**1 tsp**
2	garlic cloves, crushed	**2**	**1 tsp**	Dijon mustard	**1 tsp**
1	small sweet green pepper, seeded, deribbed and finely chopped	**1**	**1 tsp**	fresh lemon juice	**1 tsp**
			¼ tsp	salt	**¼ tsp**
				freshly ground black pepper	
			1 kg	filleted and skinned monkfish	**2¼ lb**

Push the tomatoes through the sieve with a wooden spoon to make a thin purée. Discard the pips and solids. Set the purée aside.

Heat ½ tablespoon of the oil in a saucepan and gently sweat the onion until soft but not coloured. Add the garlic and sweet green pepper, stir for a minute or two, then add the chili, tomato purée, chili powder, sugar, mustard and lemon juice.

Bring to a vigorous boil then lower to a light boil until reduced to about 35 cl (12 fl oz)—about 40 minutes. Add the salt and a little black pepper. Set aside.

Trim the monkfish and cut it into about fifty 2.5 cm (1 inch) cubes. Heat 1 tablespoon of the remaining oil in a large sauté pan and cook half of the fish pieces for 2 to 3 minutes, until just done. Lift out the fish into the sauce. Clean the pan, add the remaining oil and cook the remaining fish in the same way. Transfer to the sauce and heat through.

Pour a little sauce on to a warm serving dish. Arrange the monkfish pieces on top and then pour over any remaining sauce. Serve hot with cocktail sticks to spear the fish.

Two-Salmon Wontons

Makes 16
wontons

Working time:
about 20
minutes

Total time
about 1 hour
(includes
marinating)

Per wonton:

Calories
55

Protein
3g

Cholesterol
10mg

Total fat
2g

Saturated fat
trace

Sodium
85mg

175 g	fresh salmon steaks	**6 oz**
60 g	smoked salmon, finely chopped	**2 oz**
1 tbsp	fresh lemon juice	**1 tbsp**

1 tbsp	finely chopped fresh dill	**1 tbsp**
	freshly ground black pepper	
16	wonton wrappers	**16**

Skin the fresh salmon and remove all bones; run your fingers over the flesh to find the smaller bones, and remove these with tweezers. Finely chop the flesh and mix it together with the smoked salmon, lemon juice, dill and some black pepper. Leave to marinate for 30 minutes to 1 hour.

Place about a teaspoon of the salmon mixture in the centre of each wonton wrapper. Dip your fingertips in water and moisten the edges of each wrapper, then bring the four corners together to meet in the centre and press the edges together.

Place the wontons in a bamboo or lightly oiled stainless-steel steamer, cover and steam over boiling water until the wrappers become translucent—2 to 5 minutes. Serve immediately.

Editor's Note: If wonton wrappers are not available, you can make your own. Mix 1 egg with 4 tablespoons of water and knead with 250 g (8 oz) of sifted plain flour for 5 to 10 minutes. Divide the dough in half and roll out each half thinly into a 35 cm (14 inch) square. Trim the edges and cut each square into 16 equal pieces. The wrappers not used for this recipe may be kept in the refrigerator for up to two days, or frozen.

Sesame-Prawn Toasts

Makes 48 toasts

Working time: about 45 minutes

Total time: about 1 hour

Per toast:

Calories
15
Protein
1g
Cholesterol
5mg
Total fat
trace
Saturated fat
trace
Sodium
25mg

1 tsp	fresh lemon juice	**1 tsp**
125 g	cooked peeled prawns, finely chopped	**4 oz**
175 g	lemon sole fillets, or other white-fleshed fish	**6 oz**
2 tsp	dry vermouth	**2 tsp**
1	egg white	**1**
¼ tsp	salt	**¼ tsp**

3 tbsp	fromage frais	**3 tbsp**
3 tbsp	finely chopped spring onions	**3 tbsp**
	cayenne pepper	
6	thin slices white bread, trimmed to 9 cm (3½inch) squares	**6**
4 tsp	white sesame seeds	**4 tsp**
	lettuce leaves, for garnish	

Add the lemon juice to the chopped prawns and set the mixture aside. In a food processor, purée the fish fillets with the vermouth, egg white and salt. Transfer the mixture from the processor to a bowl and set this in a larger bowl containing ice. Beat in the fromage frais, then gently stir in the chopped spring onions, cayenne pepper and chopped prawns. Meanwhile, preheat the oven to 200°C (400°F or Mark 6).

Toast the bread under the grill until lightly browned. Spread the prawn topping over the toast and cover with an even sprinkling of sesame seeds. Cut the toast slices into quarters, then cut each quarter diagonally into two triangles. Place the triangles on a baking sheet and bake them in the oven until they are golden-brown—15 to 20 minutes. Serve the sesame-prawn toasts warm on a bed of salad leaves.

Bacon and Monkfish Rolls

Makes 18 rolls

Working time: about 15 minutes

Total time: about 45 minutes (includes marinating)

Per roll:

Calories 70

Protein 6g

Cholesterol 25mg

Total fat 5g

Saturated fat 2g

Sodium 110mg

500 g	trimmed, skinned and boned monkfish or halibut	**1 lb**
½ tsp	finely chopped fresh thyme	**½ tsp**
1	bay leaf, broken	**1**

	freshly ground black pepper	
1	lemon, juice only	**1**
9	thin rashers back bacon, trimmed of fat, cut in half lengthwise	**9**

Cut the fish into 18 cubes and put these in a bowl with the thyme, bay leaf, some pepper and the lemon juice.

Turn the cubes to coat them well and leave to marinate for at least 30 minutes. Meanwhile, soak 18 short wooden cocktail sticks in cold water for 10 minutes to prevent them from scorching under the grill.

Discard the pieces of bay leaf from the fish marinade. Wrap each cube of fish with a piece of bacon and thread on to a stick; ensure that the skewers pierce through the overlapping ends of bacon, to hold them together.

Cook the rolls under a hot grill for 4 to 5 minutes, turning once. Serve immediately.

Halibut Kievski

Makes 24 kievski

Working time: about 15 minutes

Total time: about 1 hour and 20 minutes (includes chilling)

Per kievski:

Calories 20

Protein 3g

Cholesterol 10mg

Total fat 1g

Saturated fat trace

Sodium 25mg

300 g	skinned and boned halibut or haddock, finely chopped	**10 oz**	
½ tsp	very finely grated lemon rind	**½ tsp**	
⅛ tsp	salt white pepper	**⅛ tsp**	
45 g	shelled peas, or frozen peas, thawed	**1½ oz**	
7 g	unsalted butter	**¼ oz**	
24	mange-tout (about 125 g/4 oz), strings removed	**24**	

In a food processor, combine the halibut with the lemon rind, salt and some pepper until it forms a coarse paste. Chill the paste in the refrigerator for at least 1 hour.

Parboil the peas until they are barely tender—3 to 4 minutes. Drain, refresh under cold water and drain again. (Frozen peas do not need parboiling.) Melt the butter in a small heavy-bottomed saucepan, remove from the heat and toss the peas in the butter.

Divide the paste into 24 portions. Roll a portion into a ball, then flatten it in the palm of your hand to form a disc about 7.5 cm (3

inches) in diameter. Place a few peas in the centre of the disc, then draw up the sides of the disc to form a ball around the peas. Make up more fish balls until you have used up all the paste and peas. Wrap a mange-tout round each ball and secure it with a cocktail stick.

Pour enough water into a saucepan to fill it about 2.5 cm (1 inch) deep. Set a lightly oiled stainless steel steamer in the pan and bring the water to the boil. Put the balls in the steamer, cover the pan and steam for 5 minutes. Serve immediately.

Turkey Twists

Makes 20
twists

Working time:
about 30
minutes

Total time:
about 3 hours
(includes
marinating)

Per twist:
Calories
25
Protein
5g
Cholesterol
10mg
Total fat
trace
Saturated fat
trace
Sodium
50mg

300 g	boneless turkey breasts, skinned	**10 oz**
125 g	cranberries	**4 oz**
	thinly pared lime rind, cut into 20 leaf shapes	
2 tsp	clear honey	**2 tsp**
	Lime-ginger marinade	
1 tbsp	freshly grated ginger root	**1 tbsp**
1	garlic clove, crushed	**1**
1 tbsp	clear honey	**1 tbsp**
1	lime, grated rind and 1 tbsp juice only	**1**
45 g	plain low-fat yogurt	**1½ oz**
½ tsp	salt	**½ tsp**
	Tabasco sauce	

To make the marinade, put the grated ginger, garlic, honey, grated lime rind and juice, yogurt, salt and a few drops of Tabasco sauce in a bowl and stir until evenly blended. Slice the turkey thinly, then cut into strips measuring about 12 by 1 cm (5 by ½ inch). Place the strips in the marinade, and turn to coat evenly. Set aside to marinate for 2 to 3 hours.

Soak 20 wooden kebab skewers in water for 10 to 15 minutes to prevent them from scorching under the grill during cooking.

Place the lime leaves, cranberries and honey in a small saucepan with about 2 tablespoons of water, and cook very gently until the cranberries begin to soften—3 to 4 minutes. Drain the cranberries and lime leaves and set aside.

Thread each turkey strip on to one end of a skewer to form a continuous double "S" shape, skewering a cranberry between each loop of the "S".

Line a baking sheet with non-stick parchment paper. Arrange the turkey twists on the sheet and cook under a hot grill for 12 to 15 minutes, turning once, until the turkey is tender and the coating a darker colour.

Garnish the end of each skewer with a lime leaf and arrange the twists on a serving plate.

Pork Phyllo Pastries

Makes 12
pastries

Working time:
about 20
minutes

Total time:
about 1 hour
and 10
minutes

Per pastry:
Calories
55
Protein
4g
Cholesterol
15mg
Total fat
3g
Saturated fat
2g
Sodium
15mg

300 g	pork fillet, trimmed of fat, finely chopped	**10 oz**
1 tbsp	dry sherry or rice wine	**1 tbsp**
1 tbsp	low-sodium soy sauce or shoyu	**1 tbsp**
1 tsp	finely chopped fresh ginger root	**1 tsp**

3 tbsp	chopped spring onions	**3 tbsp**
	freshly ground black pepper	
3	sheets phyllo pastry, each about 45 by 30 cm (18 by 12 inches)	**3**
30 g	unsalted butter, melted	**1 oz**

Place the chopped pork in a shallow non-reactive bowl with the sherry or rice wine, soy sauce, ginger, spring onions and some freshly ground pepper, and leave to marinate for 20 minutes.

Preheat the oven to 200°C (400°F or Mark 6). Cut each phyllo sheet into quarters and fold each quarter in half crosswise. Line 12 cups of a deep bun tin tray with the phyllo, leaving the edges to overhang. Divide the pork mixture among the cups. Brush the overhanging phyllo edges with some of the melted butter, then fold the edges over the mixture to resemble the petals of a flower; twist slightly to keep them in place. Brush the phyllo again with the remaining melted butter, then cover the tray with aluminium foil and cook in the oven for 30 minutes. About 10 minutes before the end of the cooking time, remove the foil to allow the phyllo to brown. Serve the pastries hot.

Editor's Note: These pork pastries may also be served at room temperature.

Bacon and Date Pinwheels

Makes 40
pinwheels

Working time:
about 15
minutes

Total time:
about 20
minutes

Per pinwheel:

Calories
40
Protein
2g
Cholesterol
5mg
Total fat
2g
Saturated fat
1g
Sodium
125mg

10	large thin slices wholemeal bread, crusts removed	10
10	fresh dates, halved and stoned	10
10	thin rashers lean back bacon, fat trimmed, halved lengthwise	10
1 tsp	clear honey parsley sprigs, for garnish	1 tsp

Tomato filling

300 g	tomatoes, skinned, seeded and chopped	10 oz
1 tsp	tomato paste	1 tsp
1	shallot, finely chopped	1
1	bay leaf freshly ground black pepper	1

Place all the ingredients for the tomato filling in a small heavy-bottomed saucepan. Cook over moderate heat, stirring occasionally, until the mixture has thickened. Remove from the heat and set aside.

Preheat the oven to 200°C (400°F or Mark 6). Roll out each slice of bread thinly with a rolling pin and trim into a neat rectangle with its shorter sides the length of two dates laid end to end.

Take one piece of bread and spread it sparingly with some of the tomato filling. Lay two date halves end to end along a short edge of the slice and roll up the bread firmly. Cut

the bread roll in half between the two dates. Wrap a piece of bacon round one of the rolls, cover the seam of the bread, and secure with two wooden cocktail sticks. Cut in half between the cocktail sticks to make two pinwheels. Wrap and cut the other roll.

Repeat this process to make 40 pinwheels. Place the pinwheels on a baking sheet lined with parchment paper. Warm the honey in a small saucepan and lightly brush each roll with it, then bake the pinwheels in the oven until the bacon is cooked—5 to 8 minutes. Arrange the pinwheels on a serving plate and garnish with the parsley sprigs.

Ox Heart Brochettes

Makes 16
brochettes

Working time:
about 15
minutes

Total time:
about 1 day
(includes
marinating)

Per brochette:
Calories
50
Protein
8g
Cholesterol
35mg
Total fat
2g
Saturated fat
1g
Sodium
95mg

500 g	ox heart, trimmed of fat	1 lb
5	garlic cloves, crushed	5
3	fresh red or green chili peppers, seeded, finely chopped	3
2 tsp	hot chili powder	2 tsp

2 tsp	safflower oil	2 tsp
3 tbsp	red wine vinegar	3 tbsp
½ tsp	salt	½ tsp
	freshly ground black pepper	

Cut the heart into 2.5 cm (1 inch) cubes—you should have about 48 cubes. Mix the garlic, chilies, chili powder, oil, vinegar, salt and some pepper together in a large dish. Add the ox heart cubes and turn to coat them well. Cover the dish and leave to marinate in the refrigerator for about 24 hours.

Ten minutes before grilling the ox heart, soak 16 wooden skewers, about 20 cm (8 inches) long, in water to prevent them from scorching under the grill. Preheat the grill to high. Thread the cubes of ox heart on to the skewers, reserving any marinade left in the dish, and grill the brochettes for 2 to 3 minutes on one side. Turn, brush with the reserved marinade, and cook the brochettes for a further 2 minutes. The meat should be well browned on all sides.

Editor's Note: Cubes of lean grilling steak may be substituted for the ox heart in this recipe.

Salmon and Watercress Rolls

Makes 36 rolls

Working time:
about 40
minutes

Total time:
about 2 hours
and 50 minutes
(includes
chilling)

Per roll:
Calories
50
Protein
5g
Cholesterol
15mg
Total fat
3g
Saturated fat
1g
Sodium
60mg

350 g	salmon steaks	12 oz
1	bay leaf	1
1	thyme sprig	1
1	parsley sprig	1
1	slice of lemon	1
8	black peppercorns	8
¼ tsp	salt	¼ tsp

2 tbsp	soured cream	2 tbsp
1 tsp	Dijon mustard	1 tsp
	freshly ground black pepper	
12	thin slices wholemeal bread	12
125 g	watercress, stemmed	4 oz
	washed and dried	
60 g	unsalted butter, softened	2 oz

Rinse the salmon steaks under cold water. Place them in a shallow saucepan with the herbs, lemon, peppercorns, half of the salt and 2 tablespoons of water. Cover the pan with a tightly fitting lid and simmer gently until the salmon flakes easily—8 to 10 minutes. Remove from the heat and allow the salmon to cool in the liquid for about 1 hour.

When the salmon is quite cold, carefully remove the skin and bones. Flake the flesh and put it into a bowl. Add the soured cream, mustard, the remaining salt and some pepper, and mix gently together.

Remove the crusts from the slices of bread.

Roll each slice with a rolling pin to compress the bread slightly and make it pliable.

Chop the watercress finely, then put it into a small bowl with the butter and beat well together. Spread each slice of bread thinly with the watercress butter. Divide the salmon mixture equally among the slices of bread, then spread evenly over each slice. Neatly roll up the slices of bread, like Swiss rolls, to enclose the salmon. Wrap each roll individually in plastic film to prevent drying, and refrigerate for about 1 hour. Just before serving, remove the plastic film and cut each salmon roll into three.

Vegetable Purées in Chicory

Makes about
50 leaves

Working time
about 40
minutes

Total time:
about 1 hour

Per leaf:
Calories
60
Protein
2g
Cholesterol
0mg
Total fat
2g
Saturated fat
trace
Sodium
90mg

300 g	carrots, peeled and sliced	**10 oz**
1	orange, grated rind of half, juice of whole	**1**
350 g	Brussels sprouts, trimmed	**12 oz**
350 g	potatoes, scrubbed well, dried and picked all over with a fork	**12 oz**
175 g	fromage frais	**6 oz**

1 tsp	ground coriander	**1 tsp**
¼ tsp	white pepper	**¼ tsp**
¾ tsp	salt	**¾ tsp**
1 tbsp	hazelnut oil	**1 tbsp**
¼ tsp	grated nutmeg	**¼ tsp**
1	small bunch flat-leaf parsley, chopped	**1**
4	heads chicory	**4**

Place the carrots, orange rind and juice in a dish. Cover with plastic film, leaving one corner open, and microwave on high until the carrots are tender—about 8 minutes. Cool.

Place the sprouts with 4 tablespoons of water in another dish. Cover with plastic film, leaving one corner open, and microwave on high until just soft—6 to 8 minutes. Cool.

Arrange the potatoes on paper towels in the oven. Microwave on high for about 10 minutes, turning over half way through cooking. Leave to rest for 2 minutes; if still not soft, microwave for a further 2 to 5 minutes. Cool, then remove the skins.

In a food processor chop the carrots finely.

Add 45 g (1½ oz) of *fromage frais*, the coriander, white pepper and ¼ teaspoon salt, and purée.

Remove the carrot purée from the processor and clean the bowl. Process the sprouts until finely chopped, then add the oil, nutmeg and ¼ teaspoon salt, purée. Add 30 g (1 oz) of *fromage frais* and blend. Mash the potatoes, then beat them with the parsley and the remaining *fromage frais* and salt until soft.

Separate the chicory leaves, wash and dry them carefully. Using a piping bag fitted with a large star nozzle, fill one third of the leaves with the carrot purée, one third with the sprout purée and one third with the potato purée. Arrange on a platter and serve.

Spinach and Salmon Canapés

Makes 12 canapés

Working time: about 25 minutes

Total time: about 30 minutes

Per canapé:

Calories 90

Protein 9g

Cholesterol 25mg

Total fat 4g

Saturated fat 1g

Sodium 140mg

250 g	salmon steak, skinned and boned	**8 oz**
2	egg whites	**2**
175 g	skinned sole or plaice fillets	**6 oz**
2 tbsp	quark	**2 tbsp**
6	slices wholemeal bread	**6**
1	small sweet red pepper, pricked all over with a fork	**1**
175 g	spinach leaves, stemmed, washed and drained	**6 oz**

Finely chop the salmon in a food processor, then blend in one egg white. Tip the mixture into a bowl. Repeat this procedure with the sole or plaice and the second egg white. Stir 1 tablespoon of the quark into each of the mixtures and chill them.

Place the red pepper on a paper towel in the microwave oven and microwave on high for 4 minutes, turning after every minute. Put the pepper in a small bowl, cover with plastic film and leave to cool. Peel off the skin and remove the seeds, then cut out 12 small diamond shapes from the flesh. Set aside.

Put the spinach leaves in a bowl, cover and microwave on high for 4 minutes. Drain well, taking care not to break up the leaves.

Line the hollows of two plastic egg cartons with plastic film. Divide the sole mixture equally among the 12 moulds and smooth the surface. Divide the spinach leaves into 12 portions and arrange each portion in an even layer over the sole. Top the spinach with an even layer of the salmon mixture. Cook one box at a time on high for 1½ to 2 minutes, until the fish mixtures are just firm.

Meanwhile, toast the bread and cut out 12 circles with a 4.5 cm (1¾ inch) round cutter.

Put a plate over each carton and invert it to remove the fish moulds; drain off any liquid. Lift each mould on to a circle of toast and place a red pepper diamond on top. Arrange the assembled canapés on a plate and serve them warm.

Pineapple Chunks Wrapped in Spicy Beef

Makes about
40 chunks

Working time:
about 20
minutes

Total time:
about 1 hour
and 20
minutes

Per chunk:

Calories
20

Protein
3g

Cholesterol
10mg

Total fat
1g

Saturated fat
trace

Sodium
5mg

350 g	fillet steak	**12 oz**		**1**	garlic clove, crushed	**1**
2 tbsp	sesame oil	**2 tbsp**		**½ tsp**	chili powder	**½ tsp**
2 tbsp	low-sodium soy sauce or shoyu	**2 tbsp**		**1**	pineapple	**1**

Slice the steak across the grain as thinly as possible. Halve the slices lengthwise, then stretch the pieces with the back of the knife to give strips roughly 7.5 by 1 cm (3 by ½ inch).

Put the oil, soy sauce, garlic and chili powder in a bowl. Stir in the beef slices to coat them well with the sauce. Cover the dish with plastic film and leave the meat to marinate for 1 hour, stirring twice.

Cut the top and bottom off the pineapple. Cut away the skin and slice the flesh into rings about 2 cm (¾ inch) thick. Remove the core from each slice and cut about 40 cubes from the slices.

Wrap a piece of beef round each pineapple chunk and thread on to a cocktail stick. Arrange half of the wrapped chunks on a plate, so that they are evenly spaced round the outside with their sticks pointing towards the centre. Microwave on high for 2 minutes, turning them over gently every 30 seconds. Leave to rest for 5 minutes while you cook the second batch in the same way, then serve.

Editor's Note: The chunks may also be served chilled.

Garlic Pâté

Serves 4
as a first
course

Working
time:
about 15
minutes

Total time:
about 20
minutes

Calories
140

Protein
8g

Cholesterol
trace

Total fat
6g

Saturated fat
2g

Sodium
350mg

18	large garlic cloves	18	$\frac{1}{8}$ tsp	salt	$\frac{1}{8}$ tsp
75 g	fresh wholemeal breadcrumbs	2½oz		freshly ground black pepper	
175 g	low-fat soft cheese	6 oz	1 tbsp	virgin olive oil	1 tbsp

Peel and quarter the garlic cloves. Place the pieces in a small bowl and add just enough cold water to cover them. Microwave the garlic on medium high for 3½ minutes. Drain the garlic and discard the water.

Place the garlic in a food processor or blender with half of the breadcrumbs, and blend for a few seconds. Add the remaining breadcrumbs, the low-fat soft cheese, the salt and a generous amount of black pepper, and continue to process until smooth. With the machine running, slowly dribble in the olive oil.

To serve, transfer the pâté to a serving bowl and gently smooth the surface.

Mushroom and Chestnut Pâté with Madeira

Serves 10
as a first
course

Working
time: about
30 minutes

Total time:
about
11 hours

Calories
130
Protein
4g
Cholesterol
5mg
Total fat
5g
Saturated fat
1g
Sodium
100mg

250 g	dried chestnuts, soaked overnight and drained	**8 oz**
30 g	dried mushrooms (optional)	**1 oz**
4 tbsp	Madeira	**4 tbsp**
1 tbsp	safflower oil	**1 tbsp**
750 g	button mushrooms, sliced	**1½ lb**

1 tbsp	sherry vinegar	**1 tbsp**
1 tsp	fresh thyme leaves	**1 tsp**
4½ tsp	low-sodium soy sauce ·	**4½ tsp**
	freshly ground black pepper	
2	rashers streaky bacon, rind removed	**2**
1 tbsp	chopped parsley	**1 tbsp**

Place the chestnuts in a saucepan and cover with water. Bring to the boil, cover and simmer for 30 to 45 minutes, until soft.

Soak the dried mushrooms, if you are using them, in 1 tablespoon of the Madeira and 4 tablespoons of tepid water for 20 minutes.

Drain the chestnuts, and purée in a food processor; leave in the machine. Squeeze out as much moisture as possible from the dried mushrooms; strain the soaking liquid through a double layer of muslin and set it aside. Rinse the mushrooms thoroughly in a bowl of fresh water, dry on paper towels.

Heat the oil in a large, heavy frying pan. Add the fresh mushrooms and cook until soft —about 5 minutes. Add the sherry vinegar, the dried mushrooms and their soaking liquid. Stir and cook over medium heat for 1 minute. Pour in the remaining Madeira, increase the heat and cook fast for 3 minutes to burn off the alcohol.

Add the mushroom mixture and the thyme leaves to the chestnut purée in the food processor. Process to a smooth paste. Add the soy sauce and some black pepper, and process again briefly. Transfer the pâté to a serving bowl and refrigerate it for 2 hours.

Grill the bacon until crisp. Cool, then crumble it over the top of the pâté. Sprinkle on the chopped parsley, and serve.

Chocolate and Ginger Cheesecakes

Makes 6
cheesecakes

Working time:
about 30
minutes

Total time:
about 3 hours
(includes
chilling)

Per
cheesecake:

Calories
210

Protein
10g

Cholesterol
10mg

Total fat
9g

Saturated fat
5g

Sodium
230mg

45 g	digestive biscuits	**1½ oz**	**30 g**	crystallized ginger	**1 oz**
75 g	plain chocolate	**2½ oz**	**300 g**	quark	**10 oz**
2 tsp	powdered gelatine	**2 tsp**	**6 cl**	single cream	**2 fl oz**
2 tbsp	clear honey	**2 tbsp**	**1 tsp**	icing sugar, to decorate	**1 tsp**

Cut six circles of greaseproof paper to line the bases of six 12.5 cl (4 fl oz) ramekins, using a ramekin as a guide. Break the biscuits into pieces, and process them briefly in a food processor. Break 45 g (1½ oz) of the chocolate into a basin and microwave it on medium for 2 ½ to 3 minutes, until melted. Stir until smooth, then combine with the biscuit crumbs. Divide the mixture among the ramekins, lightly pressing it into the bases. Chill until firm—about 20 minutes.

Sprinkle the gelatine over 2 tablespoons of water in a bowl and leave it to soften for 2 minutes. Microwave on high for 30 seconds, to melt the gelatine. Stir in the honey and cool slightly.

Meanwhile, very finely chop the ginger in a food processor and combine it with the quark and cream. Mix together until smooth, then, using a metal spatula, spread it out very thinly on a marble slab or an inverted baking sheet. Leave to cool for 3 to 4 minutes, until almost set. Push a pastry scraper under the chocolate to produce scrolls.

Just before serving, slip a knife round the sides of the ramekins. Carefully unmould each cheesecake into the palm of your hand—to remove the lining paper—then place it on a board. Cover the cheesecakes with chocolate scrolls. Using a metal spatula to cover half the top of each cheesecake, sift icing sugar over the half.

Chocolate-Dipped Stuffed Prunes

Makes 18
stuffed prunes

Working time
about 1 hour

Total time:
about 3 hours
(includes
setting)

Per prune:

Calories
100

Protein
1g

Cholesterol
0mg

Total fat
1g

Saturated fat
trace

Sodium
20mg

100 g	granulated sugar	**3½ oz**
15 cm	piece cinnamon stick	**6 inch**
1	vanilla pod	**1**
350 g	large prunes	**12 oz**
60 g	genoese sponge, or other plain sponge cake	**2 oz**

60 g	shelled walnuts, lightly toasted and ground	**2 oz**
4 tbsp	Armagnac or cognac	**4 tbsp**
½ tsp	pure vanilla extract	**½ tsp**
75 g	white chocolate, broken into pieces	**2½ oz**

Place the sugar in a saucepan with ¼ litre (8 fl oz) of water and heat gently until the sugar has dissolved. Add the cinnamon and vanilla pod, bring to the boil, then reduce the heat and simmer for 5 minutes. Add the prunes and simmer for 5 minutes. Using a slotted spoon, remove 18 large, well-shaped prunes and allow them to cool on a plate, then stone them carefully and open up the cavities to receive the filling. Meanwhile, the remaining prunes until very tender—20 to 40 minutes— then transfer them to a plate to cool. Discard the syrup.

For the filling, stone the soft-cooked prunes

and place in a food processor with the sponge, ground walnuts, Armagnac and vanilla extract. Process to a smooth purée. Press the filling into the prunes, and bring the sides of each prune round the filling.

Melt the chocolate in a heatproof bowl over a pan of simmering water, until it is smooth and just free of lumps but still quite thick. Dip and turn each prune in the chocolate to coat one end. Arrange the prunes, filled-side up, on a sheet of non-stick parchment paper and leave them until the chocolate has set. Serve them in petits fours cases.

Chocolate Rum Cups

Makes
12 cups

Working time:
about 30
minutes

Total time:
about 1 hour

Per cup:

Calories
105

Protein
2g

Cholesterol
trace

Total fat
5g

Saturated fat
3g

Sodium
5mg

60 g	plain chocolate, broken into pieces	**2 oz**
12	shelled hazelnuts, toasted and skinned	**12**

Chocolate rum filling

125 g	plain chocolate, broken into pieces	**4 oz**
1 tbsp	dark rum	**1 tbsp**
60 g	fromage frais	**2 oz**

First make the chocolate cups. Melt the chocolate in a heatproof bowl over a pan of simmering water until it is smooth but not runny; do not allow the chocolate to become too hot or it will be very liquid and difficult to work with. Coat the insides of 12 confectionery cases with a double layer of melted chocolate as demonstrated on the right. Chill the chocolate cups while you prepare the filling.

To make the filling, melt the chocolate in a heatproof bowl over a pan of simmering water. Remove the bowl from the heat, stir in the rum and *fromage frais* and mix to a smooth paste. Leave the filling to cool until it is firm, stirring it occasionally, then transfer it to a piping bag fitted with a 1 cm ($\frac{1}{2}$ inch) star nozzle.

Carefully peel away the confectionery cases from the chocolate cups, and pipe a whirl of the filling into each cup. Place a hazelnut on top of each whirl.

Chocolate Brandy Snaps

Makes 20
snaps

Working (and
(total) time:
about 1 hour
and 15
minutes

Per snap:
Calories
60
Protein
1g
Cholesterol
5mg
Total fat
5g
Saturated fat
3g
Sodium
5mg

60 g	unsalted butter	**2 oz**	**1 tsp**	fresh lemon juice	**1 tsp**
60 g	light brown sugar	**2 oz**	**½ tsp**	ground cinnamon	**½ tsp**
2 tbsp	golden syrup	**2 tbsp**	**150 g**	plain chocolate,	**5 oz**
60 g	plain flour, sifted	**2 oz**		broken into pieces	

Preheat the oven to 180°C (350°F or Mark 4). Grease two baking sheets and line them with non-stick parchment paper.

Put the butter, sugar and golden syrup in a small saucepan and stir them over a low heat. When the butter has melted and the sugar dissolved, remove the pan from the heat and stir in the flour. Mix until smooth, then stir in the lemon juice and cinnamon.

Drop 4 level teaspoons of the mixture on to each baking sheet, spacing them well apart. Put one sheet in the oven and bake the snaps until bubbly and golden-brown—about 10 minutes. Half way through the cooking time, put the other sheet in the oven. When the snaps on the first sheet are done, remove them from the oven and let them stand for a

minute or so. Carefully lift them off the baking sheet with a metal spatula and roll them into cylinders round the handle of a wooden spoon. Place on a wire rack.

Wipe the parchment with paper towels, refill the sheet with 4 more teaspoons of mixture and return to the oven. Remove the second sheet of cooked snaps from the oven. Let them rest briefly, then shape as before. Continue in this way. If the snaps start to harden before they are shaped, return them to the oven for a few seconds to soften.

When all the snaps are cooked and cool, melt the chocolate in a heatproof bowl set over a saucepan of hot water. Dip the ends of the snaps in the chocolate, and leave them to set on non-stick parchment paper.

Pecan-Chestnut Sweetmeats

Makes
about 25
sweetmeats

Working (and
total) time:
about 1 hour
and 15
minutes

Per sweetmeat:

Calories
45

Protein
trace

Cholesterol
0mg

Total fat
1g

Saturated fat
trace

Sodium
5mg

125 g	granulated sugar	**4 oz**		**Chestnut purée**	
2½ tbsp	fresh orange juice	**2½ tbsp**	**125 g**	chestnuts, peeled	**4 oz**
½ tsp	grated orange rind	**½ tsp**	**30 g**	light brown sugar	**1 oz**
7.5 cm	piece cinnamon stick	**3 inch**	**1 tbsp**	fresh orange juice	**1 tbsp**
60 g	shelled pecan nuts	**2 oz**	**½ tsp**	grated orange rind	**½ tsp**
	(about 50 halves)		**¼ tsp**	ground cinnamon	**¼ tsp**
			1 tbsp	brandy	**1 tbsp**

Dissolve the granulated sugar in the orange juice over a gentle heat, add the rind and cinnamon, and bring to the boil. Boil gently until a light caramel is produced, or until a sugar thermometer registers between 160°C and 170°C (320°F and 338°F). Remove the pan from the heat and place it, briefly, in a large pan of cold water to arrest the cooking process, then set it in hot water to keep the caramel fluid. Immediately coat the pecan halves by spearing their flat sides with a skewer and dipping them into the syrup; as soon as each half is coated, use a lightly oiled fork to remove it from the skewer on to non-

stick parchment paper. Leave them to harden.

To make the chestnut purée, put the chestnuts into a pan of boiling water, then reduce the heat and simmer gently until the chestnuts begin to break apart—20 to 30 minutes. Drain in a sieve. Prepare a light syrup by boiling together the brown sugar and orange juice for 2 to 3 minutes. Process the chestnuts to a powder in a food processor. Mix with the syrup, orange rind, cinnamon and brandy to a creamy consistency.

Sandwich pairs of pecan halves together with chestnut purée and place them in petits fours cases. Serve within a day of making them.

Maple Sweetmeats

Makes 30
sweetmeats

Working time:
about 30
minutes

Total time
about 1 hour
and 30
minutes

Per sweetmeat:

Calories
35
Protein
trace
Cholesterol
0mg
Total fat
2g
Saturated fat
1g
Sodium
10mg

90 g	dried apricots	**3 oz**
125 g	stoned fresh dates	**4 oz**
90 g	stoned prunes	**3 oz**
60 g	sultanas	**2 oz**

2 tbsp	maple syrup	**2 tbsp**
100 g	desiccated coconut	**3½ oz**
2 tsp	cocoa powder	**2 tsp**

Put the apricots, dates, prunes, sultanas and maple syrup into a food processor and blend until a sticky paste is formed. Turn the mixture out into a mixing bowl and add 90 g (3 oz) of the coconut. Mix the ingredients by hand to make a soft, but not sticky, paste. Divide the fruit paste into 30 equal pieces, then roll each piece into a smooth ball. Place the remaining coconut in a small dish and put the cocoa powder in another. Roll half of the fruit-paste balls in the coconut to coat them evenly, then roll the remaining balls in the cocoa powder.

Place the sweetmeats in petits fours cases and refrigerate them for about 1 hour. Serve chilled.

Editor's Note: If you do not have a food processor, pass the fruits through the fine blade of a mincer, and add the maple syrup with the coconut.

Glazed Fruits

Makes about
45 glazed
fruits

Working (and
total) time:
about 30
minutes

Per fruit:

Calories
15

Protein
trace

Cholesterol
0mg

Total fat
0g

Saturated fat
0g

Sodium
trace

8	seedless black grapes	8	8	small strawberries, hulled	8
8	seedless green grapes	8	6	raspberries	6
1	satsuma, peeled, segmented, all white pith removed from segments	1	6	Cape gooseberries	6
			175 g	granulated sugar	6 oz

Pierce each piece of fruit with a cocktail stick. Line a large baking sheet with non-stick parchment paper.

Place the sugar and 4 tablespoons of water in a small, heavy-bottomed saucepan. Set the pan over a medium heat and stir the mixture gently with a wooden spoon to dissolve the sugar. Brush down any sugar crystals stuck to the sides of the pan with a bristle pastry brush dipped in hot water. Warm a sugar thermometer in a jug of hot water and place it in the pan. Bring the syrup to the boil and boil it rapidly until it reaches the small crack stage, when the temperature on the thermometer registers between 132°C and 143°C (270°F and 290°F). At this temperature, when a little syrup is dropped from a skewer into a bowl of iced water and then removed and stretched gently between the fingers, it will separate into strands that are hard but still elastic.

Remove the syrup from the heat. Working quickly, dip the pieces of fruit, one at a time, into the syrup, then put them on the prepared baking sheet to cool and harden. Allow the syrup to set for at least 5 minutes before removing the cocktail sticks. Place each fruit in a decorative confectionery case to serve.

Editor's Note: Prepare the fruits as near as possible to serving time and keep them in a dry place. The sugar coating on the fruits quickly becomes sticky in a damp or humid atmosphere.

Fruited Turkish Coffee Squares

Makes 70
squares

Working time:
about 30
minutes

Total time:
about 1 hour
and 30
minutes

Per square
Calories
35
Protein
1g
Cholesterol
5mg
Total fat
1g
Saturated fat
0g
Sodium
25mg

250 g	plain flour	**8 oz**
1 tsp	ground cinnamon	**1 tsp**
½ tsp	ground coriander	**½ tsp**
1 tbsp	coffee beans, very finely ground	**1 tbsp**
100 g	muscovado sugar	**3½ oz**
100 g	polyunsaturated margarine	**3½ oz**
2	large bananas, peeled and very thinly sliced lengthwise	**2**

1	egg, beaten	**1**
175 g	fresh apricots, stoned and very thinly sliced	**6 oz**
½ tsp	bicarbonate of soda	**½ tsp**
½ tsp	baking powder	**½ tsp**
¼ litre	plain low-fat yogurt	**8 fl oz**
1 tbsp	icing sugar	**1 tbsp**

Preheat the oven to 200°C (400CF or Mark 6).

Sift the flour, cinnamon, coriander and coffee together in a mixing bowl. Add the muscovado sugar and rub in the margarine until fine crumbs are formed. Divide the mixture into two portions in separate bowls. Add half the beaten egg to one portion, and mix with your hands to give larger crumbs and a slightly sticky consistency. Press this mixture firmly into the base of a tin measuring about 25 by 18 cm (10 by 7 inches) and at least 4 cm (1½ inches) deep. Arrange the banana slices in rows over the crumb base, and lay rows of apricot slices on top.

Stir the bicarbonate of soda into the remaining fine crumb mixture; blend the baking powder with the remaining egg and add this and the yogurt to the crumbs. Mix well with a wooden spoon until smooth, then pour over the fruit in the tin, ensuring that the fruit is completely covered. Bake in the oven until firm to the touch—30 to 40 minutes. Remove from the oven and leave to cool in the tin.

When cool, sift the icing sugar over the top and cut into 2.5 cm (1 inch) squares to serve.

Fig and Orange Petits Fours

Makes 28 petits fours

Working time: about 40 minutes

Total time: about 1 hour

Per petit four:
Calories 45
Protein trace
Cholesterol trace
Total fat 3g
Saturated fat 1g
Sodium 10mg

30 g	unsalted butter	**1 oz**
30 g	polyunsaturated margarine	**1 oz**
1	orange, finely grated rind only	**1**
30 g	clear honey	**1 oz**
1	egg white	**1**
60 g	ground almonds	**2 oz**
30 g	cornflour, sifted	**1 oz**
30 g	plain flour, sifted	**1 oz**

30 g	stoned dates, chopped	**1 oz**
60 g	dried figs, chopped	**2 oz**
30 g	candied orange peel chopped	**1 oz**
	icing sugar (optional)	
	glacé fruits, dried fruits and candied orange peel (optional)	
	shelled pistachio nuts, skinned and chopped (optional)	

Preheat the oven to 190°C (375°F or Mark 5). Very lightly butter 28 petits fours moulds, each approximately 4 cm (1½ inches) across.

Put the butter, margarine, orange rind and honey into a mixing bowl and beat well together until light and fluffy. Gradually beat in the egg white, then fold in the ground almonds, cornflour, plain flour, chopped dates, figs and candied peel.

Fill the prepared moulds with the creamed mixture and level the tops with a round-bladed knife. Place the moulds on a baking sheet. Bake for 5 to 10 minutes until risen, lightly browned and firm to the touch. Carefully unmould on to a wire rack to cool.

Serve in petits fours cases, either plain or—as shown here—decorated with a little sifted icing sugar, glacé and dried fruits, candied peel or chopped nuts as desired.

Editor's Note: To skin pistachio nuts, drop them into boiling water and simmer for 1 minute. Drain thoroughly, then wrap them in a towel and rub them vigorously until they have shed their skins.

Cherry-Chocolate Meringue Nests

Makes 8
nests

Working
time: about
45 minutes

Total time:
about 6
hours

Per nest:
Calories
145
Protein
2g
Cholesterol
0mg
Total fat
3g
Saturated fat
2g
Sodium
15mg

2	egg whites	2	150 g	fromage frais	5 oz
125 g	caster sugar	4 oz	150 g	cherries, stoned and halved	5 oz
45 g	plain chocolate	1½ oz	3 tbsp	cherry jam	3 tbsp
1 tbsp	kirsch	1 tbsp	1 tsp	arrowroot	1 tsp

Preheat the oven to 100°C (200°F or Mark ¼). Line a baking sheet with non-stick parchment paper and, using an oval cutter as a guide, pencil eight 7.5 by 5 cm (3 by 2 inch) ovals on to the paper; leave at least 2.5 cm (1 inch) between ovals. Turn the paper over.

Put the egg whites and sugar into a large bowl over a pan of simmering water, taking care that the bowl does not touch the water. Stir with a whisk until the sugar has dissolved and the egg whites are hot—about 4 minutes—then whisk more vigorously until the meringue is stiff and glossy.

Spoon the meringue into a piping bag fitted with a 1 cm (½ inch) star nozzle, and make bases for the nests by filling in the ovals on the baking paper with coils of meringue. To make the sides of the nests, pipe two layers—one on top of the other—round the edge of each base. Bake the nests until crisp and dry, but not brown—5 to 6 hours. Cool on a wire rack.

Melt the chocolate in a heatproof bowl set over a pan of simmering water. Carefully paint the base inside each nest with a thin layer of melted chocolate.

Beat the kirsch into the *fromage frais* and, when the chocolate has set, spoon it into the nests. Top with the halved cherries.

In a small, saucepan, melt the jam with 2 tablespoons of water. Sieve to remove any solids, then stir in the arrowroot. Return to the pan and bring to the boil, stirring. Remove from the heat and allow the glaze to thicken before brushing it over the cherries in each nest.

Cocktail Croutons

Makes about 200 croutons

Working time: about 30 minutes

Total time about 45 minutes

Per 5 croutons:

Calories 40

Protein 1g

Cholesterol 4mg

Total fat 2g

Saturated fat 1g

Sodium 4mg

12	thin slices day-old wholemeal bread, about 12 by 10 cm (5 by 4 inches) each	**12**
60 g	unsalted butter	**2 oz**
1 tbsp	Dijon mustard	**1 tbsp**
2	garlic cloves, crushed	**2**
2 tbsp	finely chopped parsley	**2 tbsp**
¼ tsp	salt	**¼ tsp**
⅛ tsp	cayenne pepper	**⅛ tsp**
30 g	Parmesan cheese, finely grated	**1 oz**

Preheat the oven to 220°C (425°F or Mark 7). Grease several baking sheets.

Remove the crusts from the bread. Put the butter into a bowl with the mustard, crushed garlic, chopped parsley, salt and cayenne pepper. Beat together until the mixture is very soft and creamy.

Spread both sides of each slice of bread very thinly with the savoury butter. Sprinkle one side of each slice of bread with the grated Parmesan, then cut each slice into about 18 small triangles, as shown here, or into squares or oblongs.

Put the bread shapes on the baking sheets and cook in the oven until they are crisp and golden-brown—10 to 15 minutes. Serve warm or cold.

Oatmeal Cheese Straws

Makes about 100 straws

Working (and total) time: about 1 hour

Pet 5 straws:
Calories 65
Protein 2g
Cholesterol 20mg
Total fat 5g
Saturated fat 2g
Sodium 90mg

60 g	rolled oats	**2 oz**
60 g	plain flour	**2 oz**
½ tsp	baking powder	**½ tsp**
¼ tsp	salt	**¼ tsp**
½ tsp	dry mustard	**½ tsp**
¼ tsp	cayenne pepper	**¼ tsp**

60 g	polyunsaturated margarine	**2 oz**
60 g	Cheddar cheese, finely grated	**2 oz**
30 g	parmesan cheese, finely grated	**1 oz**
1	egg beaten	**1**
	skimmed milk	

Preheat the oven to 200°C (400°F or Mark 6). Grease several baking sheets

Finely grind the oats in a food processor. Sift the flour, baking powder, salt, mustard and cayenne pepper into a bowl. Add the oats, and rub in the margarine until the mixture resembles fine breadcrumbs. Add the Cheddar, half of the Parmesan and the egg. Mix to a soft dough. Knead lightly on a floured surface.

Roll the dough out to an oblong about 30 by 22 cm (12 by 9 inches). Trim the edges and, resere the trimmings. Brush with a little milk and sprinkle on the remaining Parmesan cheese. Cut into three equal strips lengthwise, then cut across each strip to make 5 mm (¼ inch) wide straws. Place on the baking sheets, spaced slightly apart. Bake in the oven until golden brown—10 to 15 minutes. Carefully remove the straws to wire racks to cool.

Re-knead and roll out the reserved trimmings. Using a 5 cm (2 inch) plain cutter, cut out rounds from the dough, then, using a 3 cm (1¼ inch) plain cutter, cut out the centre from each round to make a ring. Place on a baking sheet. Re-knead and roll out the trimmings and repeat process until the pastry is used up. Bake for 6 to 8 minutes, until golden-brown. Remove to wire racks to cool.

To serve, fill each ring with straws and arrange them on a serving platter.

Labne Cocktail Balls

Makes about
24 labne balls

Working time:
about 20
minutes

Total time:
about 26 hours
(includes
draining)

Per 3 balls

Calories
70

Protein
3g

Cholesterol
10mg

Total fat
3g

Saturated fat
2g

Sodium
35mg

500 g	unstirred and unstrained ewe's milk yogurt	**1 lb**
2 tsp	coriander seeds, toasted and lightly crushed	**2 tsp**
2 tbsp	medium-grade oatmeal toasted	**2 tbsp**

2 tsp	black poppy seeds, toasted	**2 tsp**
4 tbsp	finely chopped mixed fresh herbs such as parsley, chervil, mint, tarragon and lemon balm	**4 tbsp**

To make the labne, line a large sieve with a single layer of dampened muslin. Place the sieve over a deep bowl and gently spoon the yogurt into the sieve.

Cover the bowl and sieve with plastic film and set aside for about 2 hours to start the initial separation of curds and whey. Then put the sieve and bowl into the refrigerator and let the yogurt continue draining for about 24 hours to form a firm thick curd in the sieve.

When the labne is ready, add the crushed coriander seeds and mix well. Place the oatmeal on a shallow plate, the poppy seeds on another and the fresh herbs on a third. Using a melon baller, miniature ice-cream scoop or two teaspoons, make small balls of curd and drop some on to each of the three coatings. Carefully roll the balls until they are well coated, then arrange them on a serving dish and refrigerate until required.

Editor's Note: Labne may be made in advance and kept in the refrigerator, covered with plastlc film, for two or three days. To toast coriander and poppy seeds, place them in a heavy-bottomed pan over high heat and cook until they darken slightly, bounce and release their aroma—1 to 2 minutes. Shake the pan to keep the seeds moving Toast oatmeal in the same way until golden.

Stuffed Cherry Tomatoes

Makes
about 20
stuffed
tomatoes

Working (and
total) time:
about 30
minutes

Per stuffed
tomato:
Calories
20
Protein
1g
Cholesterol
trace
Total fat
2g
Saturated fat
0g
Sodium
25mg

250 g	cherry tomatoes	8 oz	⅛ tsp	salt	⅛ tsp
125 g	medium-fat curd cheese	4 oz		freshly ground black pepper	
2 tsp	chopped fresh basil	2 tsp		parsley leaves, for garnish	

Slice the bottoms off the tomatoes and, using a small vegetable baller or a teaspoon, scoop out the seeds and juice into a sieve placed over a small bowl. Press the juice from the seeds and discard the seeds. Mix the cheese with the chopped basil, salt, a little freshly ground pepper and about 3 teaspoons of the tomato juice, to make a soft paste.

Using a piping bag fitted with a 1 cm (½ inch) star nozzle, pipe a rosette of the curd cheese mixture into each tomato. Garnish each filled tomato with a tiny piece of parsley, and arrange them on a serving plate.

Lemon and Tarragon Scallop Croustades

Makes 24
croustades

Working time:
about 20
minutes

Total time:
about 30
minutes

Per croustade

Calories
20
Protein
1g
Cholesterol
5mg
Total fat
1g
Saturated fat
0g
Sodium
45mg

6 slices	wholemeal bread	**6 slices**	**½ tsp**	grated lemon rind	**½ tsp**
15 g	polyunsaturated margarine, melted	**½ oz**	**½ tsp**	fresh lemon juice	**½ tsp**
	Lemon and tarragon filling		**1 tsp**	finely chopped fresh tarragon	**1 tsp**
				freshly ground black pepper	
6	scallops, bright white connective tissue removed, liquor from shells reserved	**6**	**1 tsp**	single cream	**1 tsp**
				fresh tarragon sprigs, for garnish	
4 tsp	arrowroot	**4 tsp**		thin strips of lemon rind, for garnish	

Preheat the oven to 220°C (425°F or Mark 7).

For the cases, flatten the slices of bread with a rolling pin. Using a 6 cm (2 ½ inch) shaped cutter, cut out 24 shapes. Brush 24 small bun tins, about 4 cm (1 ½ inches) in diameter, with some margarine, and press the bread into the moulds. Brush the bread cases with the remaining margarine, and bake them in the oven until browned—about 10 minutes.

For the filling, strain the liquor from the scallop shells into a measuring jug, and make up to 15 cl (¼ pint) with cold water. Place the arrowroot in a small bowl and blend it with 2 tablespoons of the liquid.

Pour the remaining liquid into a small pan and bring to the boil; add the scallops and simmer, covered, for 2 minutes. Remove the scallops, dice them and set aside.

Pour the arrowroot mixture into the liquid and stir. Add the grated lemon rind and juice, tarragon and some pepper. Bring to the boil and cook for 1 minute, then remove from the heat and stir in the cream and scallops.

Arrange the bread cases on a serving plate. Divide the filling among them, and garnish with the tarragon sprigs and lemon rind. Serve at room temperature.

Herb Popcorn

Makes
1 bowl

Working time
about 15
minutes

Total time
about 20
minutes

Calories
555

Protein
18g

Cholesterol
40mg

Total fat
34g

Saturated fat
10g

Sodium
100mg

2 tsp	safflower oil	**2 tsp**
175 g	popping corn	**6 oz**
	Herb flavouring	
15 g	unsalted butter	**½ oz**
1	garlic clove, crushed	**1**

1 tbsp	freshly chopped mixed herbs, such as basil, parsley and chervil	**1 tbsp**
2 tsp	freshly grated Parmesan cheese	**2 tsp**
2 tbsp	pumpkin seeds	**2 tbsp**

To prepare the herb flavouring, melt the butter in a heavy-bottomed saucepan, then add the garlic, herbs, Parmesan cheese and pumpkin seeds. Cook, stirring continuously, for 1 minute, then set aside.

While the flavourings are hot, heat the oil in a large, heavy-bottomed saucepan, add the popping corn and cover. Heat gently, shaking the pan, until all the corn has popped—2 to 3 minutes; discard any unpopped corn. Tip about one third of the popcorn into each of the flavourings and stir until evenly coated. When you stir the popcorn into the spice flavouring, add also the sesame seeds. Put the popcorn into separate bowls and serve immediately, while still warm.

Plantain Crisps

Serves 10

Total time:
about 50
minutes

Calories
110
Protein
1g
Cholesterol
0mg
Total fat
6g
Saturated fat
1g
Sodium
trace

4	large green plantains	4	**4 tbsp** safflower oil	**4 tbsp**

Top and tail the plantains with a stainless steel knife. Slit the skin of each plantain lengthwise into quarters, then peel off the strips of skin.

With a lightly oiled knife, slice the plantains as thinly as possible. Place the slices in a bowl of salted water and set aside for about 30 minutes, then drain them and pat them dry.

Heat the oil in a non-stick frying pan over medium heat and fry the first batch of plantain slices for $1\frac{1}{2}$ to 2 minutes, turning once, until they are golden-brown. Cook the remaining slices in the same way. As each batch is cooked, remove the slices from the pan with a slotted spoon and lay them on paper towels to absorb any excess fat. Serve the plantain crisps hot, in a lined basket or on a large plate.

Aubergine Sausages

Makes about 40 sausages

Working time: about 1 hour

Total time. about 1 hour and 30 minutes (includes soaking)

Per sausage:

Calories
35

Protein
2g

Cholesterol
5mg

Total fat
2g

Saturated fat
1g

Sodium
65mg

750 g	aubergines	**1½ lb**
250 g	potatoes, peeled and chopped	**8 oz**
175 g	fresh brown breadcrumbs	**6 oz**
125 g	low-fat soft cheese	**4 oz**
1	egg, lightly beaten	**1**
2	shallots, finely chopped	**2**
2 tsp	tomato paste	**2 tsp**
1 tbsp	chopped parsley	**1 tbsp**
1 tbsp	chopped fresh rosemary	**1 tbsp**
1 tsp	grated nutmeg	**1 tsp**
½ tsp	salt	**½ tsp**

	freshly ground black pepper	
2 metres	lamb sausage casing, soaked in acidulated water for 1 hour	**6 feet**
1 tsp	safflower oil	**1 tsp**
2 tsp	clear honey	**2 tsp**
	Green peppercorn dip	
250 g	fromage frais	**8 oz**
2 tsp	green peppercorns	**2 tsp**
2 tbsp	chopped capers	**2 tbsp**
1 tbsp	chopped fresh tarragon	**1 tbsp**
2 tsp	tarragon vinegar	**2 tsp**

Preheat the oven to 220°C (425°F or Mark 7). Halve the aubergines lengthwise and place, cut side down, on a foil-lined baking sheet. Bake until tender—20 to 30 minutes.

Cook the potatoes in boiling water until almost tender. Drain them and set aside.

Remove the aubergines from the oven, but leave the oven on. Scoop out the flesh and purée with the potatoes, breadcrumbs and soft cheese. Add the egg, shallots, tomato paste, herbs, nutmeg, salt and pepper, until blended.

Unravel the sausage casings and cut in two. Rinse both the casings with water, then drain. Form the 2.5 cm (1 inch) sausages, place the on a baking sheet and brush with oil. Bake for 12 to 15 minutes, until golden-brown.

Mix together the ingredients for the dip. Then gently warm the honey in a small pan.

Allow the cooked sausages to cool slightly before cutting through the links. Brush the sausages with the warmed honey and serve hot with the green peppercorn dip.

Goujons with Dill and Gherkin Dip

Serves 10
Working time about 20 minutes

Total time about 30 minutes

Calories
95
Protein
9g
Cholesterol
40mg
Total fat
4g
Saturated fat
3g
Sodium
65mg

125 g	medium oatmeal	**4 oz**
1	egg white	**1**
1 tsp	fresh lemon juice	**1 tsp**
1 tbsp	wholemeal flour	**1 tbsp**
¼ tsp	salt	**¼ tsp**
	freshly ground black pepper	
350 g	plaice fillets, skinned	**12 oz**

	Dill and gherkin dip	
175 g	crème fraîche	**6 oz**
175 g	thick Greek yogurt	**6 oz**
2	baby gherkins, finely chopped	**2**
1 tsp	finely cut fresh dill	**1 tsp**
	lemon, grated rind only	
	freshly ground black pepper	
	dill sprig, for garnish	

Preheat the oven to 220°C (425°F or Mark 7).

Put the oatmeal on a baking sheet and toast in the oven until it is golden-brown—10 to 15 minutes; stir once or twice during this time, checking that the oatmeal does not burn. Remove it from the oven and allow it to cool.

To prepare the dip, mix together the *crème fraîche*, Greek yogurt, chopped gherkins, cut dill, lemon rind and some pepper. Transfer to a serving bowl and garnish with the sprig of dill.

Lightly whisk together the egg white and lemon juice; mix the oatmeal with the flour, salt and some pepper. Cut the plaice fillets into strips about 7.5 by 1 cm (3 by ½ inch). Dip the strips in the egg white, shake off excess, then roll them in the oatmeal mixture, coating them evenly. Place the strips on a non-stick baking sheet, and cook in the oven until the fish is tender and the outside lightly browned—3 to 5 minutes Serve the goujons hot, accompanied by the dip.

Stuffed Pasta Rings

Makes 24 rings

Working time: about 20 minutes

Total time: about 30 minutes

Per ring:

Calories 40

Protein 2g

Cholesterol trace

Total fat 1g

Saturated fat trace

Sodium 70mg

4	thin slices wholemeal bread, crusts removed	4
3	cannelloni tubes (about 60 g/2 oz)	3
90 g	low-fat mozzarella, grated	3 oz
3 tbsp	medium oatmeal	3 tbsp
30 g	very thinly sliced prosciutto, flat-leaf parsley, for garnish	1 oz

Tomato and basil filling

4	spring onions, finely chopped	4
1	small garlic clove, crushed	1
300 g	tomatoes, skinned, chopped	10 oz
2 tsp	tomato paste	2 tsp
1 tsp	finely chopped fresh basil	1 tsp
½ tsp	clear honey freshly ground black pepper	½ tsp

To prepare the tomato and basil filling, place the spring onions, garlic, tomatoes and tomato paste in a small, heavy saucepan. Cook, stirring until pulpy and thick. Stir in the basil, honey and a little pepper. Set aside.

Roll out the slices of bread thinly, then cut six rounds from each slice using a 2.5 cm (1 inch) plain cutter. Toast until browned Arrange evenly, spaced apart, on a baking sheet.

Cook the cannelloni in plenty of lightly salted boiling water until just tender—8 to 10 minutes. Drain and rinse well, then thread each pasta tube on to a wooden spoon handle.

Mix the mozzarella and oatmeal. Using the round cutter, cut out 24 rounds of prosciutto; set the rounds aside for garnish.

Cut each pasta tube into eight rings and place the rings on the toast rounds. Divide the mozzarella and oatmeal mixture into two, distribute one portion among the pasta rings. Divide the tomato filling equally among the pasta rings, then sprinkle with the remaining mozzarella mixture. Place under a hot grill until the mozzarella topping begins to brown.

Garnish each canapé with a folded piece of prosciutto and a parsley leaf.

Sausage Rolls

Makes
40 rolls

Working time:
about 1 hour

Total time:
about 1 hour
and 25
minutes

Per roll

Calories
50

Protein
2g

Cholesterol
5mg

Total fat
3g

Saturated fat
1g

Sodium
80mg

20	thin slices wholemeal bread	20
2 tbsp	prepared English or	2 tbsp
	Dijon mustard	
60 g	polyunsaturated margarine	2 oz
2 tsp	tomato paste	2 tsp
2	garlic cloves, crushed	2
	Pork sausage-meat	
1	onion, roughly chopped	1

400 g	pork shoulder, trimmed	14 oz
	of excess fat	
60 g	fresh wholemeal breadcrumbs	2 oz
30 g	polyunsaturated margarine	1 oz
¼ tsp	salt	¼ tsp
	freshly ground black pepper	
2 tsp	mixed dried herbs	2 tsp

To make the sausage-meat, cut the pork into strips and pass the meat and onion through the fine blade of a mincer into a bowl. Mix in the breadcrumbs, margarine, salt, pepper and herbs. Pass through the mincer once again.

Preheat the oven to 220°C (425°F or Mark 7). Grease several baking sheets.

Cut the crusts from the bread and roll each slice with a rolling pin, until pliable. Set aside.

Divide the sausage-meat mixture into five equal portions, then shape each portion. into a sausage shape about 40 cm (16 inches) long Cut each sausage into four equal pieces.

Spread each slice of bread with the mustard. Put a length of meat on one edge of each slice. Roll the bread to enclose the meat, ending with the join underneath.

Put the margarine, tomato paste and garlic into a small bowl and beat well together until very soft. Brush the garlic mixture evenly over the sausage rolls. Cut each roll in half. Place the sausage rolls, seam side down, on the prepared baking sheets and cook in the oven until they are golden-brown and crisp—about 25 minutes. Serve warm.

Pink Trout Mousse

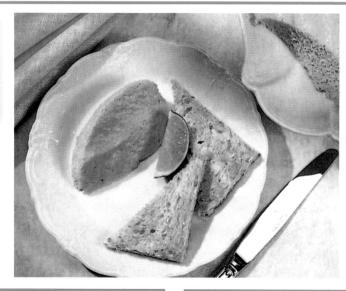

Serves 12
as a first
course

Working time:
about 30
minutes

Total time:
about 4 hours
(includes
chilling)

Calories
75

Protein
12g

Cholesterol
25mg

Total fat
2g

Saturated fat
trace

Sodium
120mg

2	shallots, finely chopped	2
30 cl	unsalted fish stock	½ pint
½	lime, juice only	½
2 tbsp	dry vermouth	2 tbsp
500 g	trout fillets	1 lb
1 tbsp	tomato paste	1 tbsp

90 g	thick Greek yogurt	3 oz
½ tsp	salt	½ tsp
	white pepper	
1 tbsp	powdered gelatine	1 tbsp
3	egg whites	3
¼	cucumber, sliced, for garnish	¼

Place the shallots in a large, shallow pan with the fish stock, lime juice and vermouth. Bring the liquid to the boil, reduce the heat and simmer gently for 3 minutes, until the shallots have softened. Lay the trout fillets in the stock, skin side down. Cover the pan and simmer for 3 minutes, then remove from the heat and leave the fish to cool in the stock.

Lift out the fish from the pan. Roughly flake the fish, discarding the skin and any bones. Strain the stock. Place the fish in a food processor, together with the strained stock, and blend the ingredients until smooth. Turn out the mixture into a bowl and beat in the tomato paste, yogurt, salt and some pepper.

Dissolve the gelatine in 3 tablespoons of cold water. Slowly pour the dissolved gelatine over the fish mixture, beating it well all the time. Chill the fish mixture until it is just beginning to set—15 to 20 minutes.

Whisk the egg whites until they are stiff but not dry. Using a large metal spoon, stir one third of the egg whites into the fish mixture to lighten it, then gently fold in the remaining egg whites; avoid overmixing. Turn the mousse into a dampened serving dish and chill it until it is set—about 3 hours.

Serve the mousse garnished with the cucumber.

Artichoke-Stuffed Mushrooms

Makes 20 stuffed mushrooms

Working time: about 30 minutes

Total time: about 40 minutes

Per mushroom:
Calories 20
Protein trace
Cholesterol 0mg
Total fat 2g
Saturated fat 1g
Sodium 35mg

20	open cup mushrooms, wiped clean, stems removed	20	$\frac{1}{2}$ tsp	Dijon mustard	$\frac{1}{2}$ tsp
1	lemon, juice only	1	$\frac{1}{4}$ tsp	salt	$\frac{1}{4}$ tsp
30 g	polyunsaturated margarine	1 oz		freshly ground black pepper	
	Artichoke stuffing		1	garlic clove, crushed	1
4	small, or two large, artichokes trimmed down to the hearts, chokes removed	4	$\frac{1}{4}$ tsp	ground cardamom	$\frac{1}{4}$ tsp
			1 tbsp	virgin olive oil	1 tbsp
2 tsp	red wine vinegar	2 tsp	1 tbsp	chopped flat-leaf parsley, plus flat-leaf parsley sprigs for garnish	1 tbsp

Put the stemmed mushrooms into a large bowl with the lemon juice. Toss them gently together, and set aside for 5 to 10 minutes.

Cook the artichoke hearts in boiling water until tender—5 to 6 minutes. Drain in a colander and refresh under cold running water. Drain and set aside.

Melt the margarine in a wide sauté pan or heavy frying pan with a lid. Place the mushrooms in a single layer in the pan, rounded sides down. Cover and cook until they just begin to soften—2 to 3 minutes do

not overcook, as they will lose their shape). Lift out the mushrooms from the pan on to paper towels to drain and cool.

For the stuffing, put the vinegar, mustard, salt, some pepper, garlic, cardamom, oil and chopped parsley into a bowl and whisk together. Finely chop the artichoke hearts and add them to the bowl. Mix well.

Spoon the mixture into the mushrooms, mounding it neatly. Garnish each one with a tiny sprig of parsley, then arrange the mushrooms neatly on a serving dish.

Pasta, Corn and Leek Salad

Serves 6 as a side dish

Working time: about 20 minutes

Total time: about 30 minutes

Calories
260

Protein
10g

Cholesterol
0mg

Total fat
4g

Saturated fat
1g

Sodium
110mg

90 g	pasta spirals	**3 oz**
4	ears of sweetcorn, husked, or 500 g (1 lb) frozen sweetcorn kernels	**4**
250 g	white parts of leek, cut into thin rounds	**8 oz**
2	beef tomatoes, cut into thin wedges	**2**
2	black olives, stoned and diced	**2**

Mustard-basil dressing		
1 tbsp	fresh lemon juice	**1 tbsp**
1 tsp	Dijon mustard	**1 tsp**
100 g	low-fat fromage frais	**3½ oz**
¼ tsp	salt	**¼ tsp**
	freshly ground black pepper	
4 tbsp	chopped fresh basil	**4 tbsp**

Cook the pasta spirals in 1 litre (1¾ pints) of boiling water with 1 teaspoon of salt. Start testing the pasta after 10 minutes and continue cooking it until it is *al dente*. Rinse the pasta under running water, then drain.

If you are using fresh sweetcorn, cook it in a saucepan of boiling water for 6 to 10 minutes, until it is just tender. Refresh the ears under cold running water and drain them well. Using a sharp knife, cut off the corn kernels. If you are using frozen sweetcorn, blanch it in boiling water and drain it thoroughly.

Parboil the leeks for 2 to 3 minutes, until still have bite. Refresh them under cold

running water and drain them well.

For the dressing, blend the lemon juice and mustard into the fromage frais, then stir in the salt, some pepper and the chopped basil. Tip the pasta, sweetcorn and leeks into a lidded plastic container, pour on the dressing and toss the salad gently to combine the ingredients. Chill the salad until required.

Put the container of dressed salad in a cool box to transport it to the picnic site. Pack the tomato wedges and olive dice in separate small containers and carry these in the cool box too. To serve, arrange the tomato wedges round the edge of a serving bowl, pile the salad in the centre and sprinkle over the olive dice.

Feta and Phyllo Parcels

Makes 12 parcels

Working time: about 30 minutes

Total time: about 45 minutes

Per parcel:

Calories 75

Protein 2g

Cholesterol 5mg

Total fat 6g

Saturated fat 1g

Sodium 130mg

4	sheets phyllo pastry, each about 45 by 30 cm (18 by 12 inches)	**4**
3 tbsp	virgin olive oil	**3 tbsp**
125 g	feta cheese, rinsed, patted dry and cut into 12 pieces	**4 oz**
1 tbsp	finely chopped fresh mint	**1 tbsp**

Preheat the oven to 180°C (350°F or Mark 4).

Place one sheet of phyllo pastry on the worktop and brush a little of the olive oil on its upper surface. Then place a second phyllo sheet on top of the first and brush its upper surface with oil. Turn the two sheets over together and brush the upper surface. (Meanwhile, keep the other two sheets of the phyllo pastry covered with a damp cloth to prevent them from drying out and becoming brittle.)

Using a saucer about 15 cm (6 inches) in diameter as a template, cut out six discs from the double sheet of oiled phyllo. Place a piece of feta cheese and a little chopped fresh mint in the centre of each disc. Gather up the phyllo edges carefully and twist them slightly to make a frill resembling a toffee wrapper. Transfer the phyllo parcels to a baking tin. Repeat with the remaining two phyllo sheets.

Bake the phyllo parcels on the lower shelf of the oven for 5 minutes, then reduce the oven temperature to 170°C (325°F or Mark 3) and bake the parcels until the bottoms and sides are evenly coloured—a further 10 to 15 minutes. Transfer them to a warm serving platter and serve at once.

Mange-Tout with Purée

Makes about
18 mange-tout

Working time:
about 30
minutes

Total time
about 45
minutes

Per 3 Carrot
mange-tout:

Calories
25

Protein
2g

Cholesterol
0mg

Total fat
trace

Saturated fat
trace

Sodium
20mg

125 g	mange-tout	4 oz
	Cumin-scented carrot purée	
125 g	carrots, peeled and sliced into 5 mm (¼ inch) rounds	4 oz
¼ tsp	ground cumin	¼ tsp

1 tbsp	fromage frais	1 tbsp
2 tsp	fresh breadcrumbs	2 tsp
⅛ tsp	salt	⅛ tsp
	white pepper	

Place the mange-tout in a deep, heatproof bowl and pour a kettle of boiling water over them. Drain immediately in a colander and refresh under cold running water. Leave the mange-tout in the colander to drain.

To make the carrot purée, put the carrots into a saucepan with cold water to barely cover, add the cumin, bring to the boil and cook until the carrots are soft—15 to 20 minutes. Drain over a bowl. Return the cooking liquid to the pan and reduce over high heat until only about a teaspoonful remains. Purée the carrots with the reduced cooking liquid in a blender, food processor or

vegetable mill. If a smoother texture is preferred, pass the purée through a fine-meshed sieve. If the purée is watery, cook it briefly in a saucepan over very low heat to dry it out a little. Stir in the *fromage frais* and breadcrumbs, season with the salt and some pepper, then set the mixture aside.

Arrange the mange-tout on serving dishes. Using a piping bag fitted with a fine nozzle, pipe the carrot purée in a line down the centre of half of the mange-tout. Then pipe the pea purée on to the remaining mange-tout. Serve cold.

Sigara Borek with Asparagus and Parmesan

Makes 12
sigara

Working time:
about 15
minutes

Total time:
about 30
minutes

Per sigara:
Calories
20
Protein
1g
Cholesterol
trace
Total fat
1g
Saturated fat
trace
Sodium
15 mg

12	asparagus spears, trimmed and peeled	12
2	sheets phyllo pastry, each about 45/ 30 cm (18 by 12 inches)	2
3 tsp	freshly grated, Parmesan cheese freshly ground black pepper	3 tsp
½ tbsp	virgin olive oil	½ tbsp

Trim the asparagus spears to about 10 cm (4 inches) long, discarding any excess stalk. Cook the spears in boiling water for 3 minutes, then drain them in a colander and refresh under cold running water. Drain the spears well and pat then dry with paper towels.

Preheat the oven to 200°C (400°F or Mark 6).

Lay out the sheets of phyllo pastry on a lightly floured board. Cut each in half lengthwise, then across three times to make 12 squares about 15 by 15 cm (6 by 6 inches). Sprinkle the phyllo squares evenly with the Parmesan cheese.

Keeping the phyllo you are not working on covered with a damp cloth to prevent it from drying out, lay an asparagus spear on a phyllo square, about 2.5 cm (1 inch) in from one edge, and sprinkle with a little black pepper. Fold the edge over the asparagus, then fold in the two adjacent sides at a slight angle, so that the side of the square opposite the spear is narrower. Roll up the spear into a neat cigarette shape and brush each one with a little of the oil. Make the remaining asparagus rolls in the same way.

Bake the sigara in the oven for 10 to 15 minutes, turning once so that they brown evenly. Serve hot.

Veal with Apricot and Nut Stuffing

Makes 32 slices

Working time about 15 minutes

Total time: about 1 hour and 25 minutes (includes soaking)

Per slice:

Calories 45
Protein 5g
Cholesterol 15mg
Total fat 2g
Saturated fat 1g
Sodium 40mg

4	veal escalopes (175 g/6 oz each), beaten thin	4
1 tsp	safflower oil	1 tsp
	coriander sprigs, for garnish	
	Apricot and nut stuffing	
125 g	dried apricots, soaked in boiling water for at least 1 hour, chopped	4 oz
1 tbsp	finely chopped spring onion	1 tbsp
60 g	unsalted cashew nuts, finely chopped	2 oz
2 tsp	chopped fresh coriander	2 tsp
6	cardamom pods, crushed, seeds only	6
4 tbsp	fresh orange juice	4 tbsp
¼ tsp	salt	¼ tsp
	freshly ground black pepper	

Preheat the oven to 200°C (400°F or Mark 6). Line a baking sheet with non-stick parchment paper.

To make the stuffing, place the chopped apricots, spring onion, cashew nuts, coriander, cardamom seeds, orange juice, salt and some freshly ground pepper in a heavy-bottomed saucepan. Cook over a moderate heat, stirring occasionally, until the mixture softens—about 2 minutes.

Cut the veal escalopes in half across their width. Divide the stuffing among the pieces of veal, spreading it evenly to the edges. Neatly roll up each piece and secure it with two cocktail sticks or small skewers. Place the rolls on the baking sheet and lightly brush the meat with the oil.

Bake the stuffed rolls in the centre of the oven until the veal is lightly browned—5 to 8 minutes. Allow the rolls to cool for a few minutes, then remove the cocktail sticks and cut each roll into four slices. Serve immediately, garnished with the coriander sprigs.

Liver and Fruit Pâté

Serves 16 as a first course

Total time about 3 days (includes chilling)

Calories 150
Protein 10g
Cholesterol 110mg
Total fat 6g
Saturated fat 2g
Sodium 435mg

125 g	dried apricots, chopped	**4 oz**
125 g	stoned prunes, chopped	**4 oz**
4	oranges, juice only	**4**
2 tbsp	virgin olive oil	**2 tbsp**
2	large onions, finely chopped	**2**
500 g	pig's liver, sliced	**1 lb**
90 g	thin rashers green streaky bacon rinds removed, chopped	**3 oz**
2 tbsp	chopped fresh thyme	**2 tbsp**
2	large cooking apples, peeled, cored and roughly chopped	**2**
2 tbsp	chopped flat-leaf parsley	**2 tbsp**
125 g	fresh brown breadcrumbs	**4 oz**
1	lemon, juice only	**1**
2	eggs, beaten	**2**
1 tbsp	green peppercorns, crushed	**1 tbsp**

Place the dried fruit in a bowl. Pour in the orange juice, and leave to soak overnight.

Heat the oil in a large saucepan over medium heat. Add the onions and cook until transparent—about 5 minutes. Add the liver and chopped bacon, and cook, stirring, until the liver is evenly browned—about 10 minutes. Mix in the apple, thyme and parsley, and cook for a further 2 to 3 minutes. Remove from the heat, allow to cool slightly, then transfer to a food processor. Add the breadcrumbs, lemon juice and eggs, and process to a smooth pâté. Turn into a bowl, then stir in the prunes and apricots with any unabsorbed orange juice. Add the green peppercorns, and mix lightly.

Preheat the oven to 180°C (350°F or Mark 4). Line a 22 by 10 by 6 cm (9 by 4 by 2½ inch) terrine or loaf tin with parchment paper and spoon in the pâté, pressing it down. Cover the terrine tightly with foil. Place in a large roasting pan and pour in boiling water to come two thirds of the way up the side of the tin. Bake until firm to the touch—about 1½ hours. Leave to cool then weight with a 500 g (1 lb) weight. Chill for at least 8 hours or overnight. Remove the weight, cover the pâté and leave to refrigerate for two more days. Turn out the pâté and serve cut into slices.

Useful weights and measures

Weight Equivalents

Avoirdupois		Metric
1 ounce	=	28.35 grams
1 pound	=	254.6 grams
2.3 pounds	=	1 kilogram

Liquid Measurements

$1/4$ pint	=	$1^1/2$ decilitres
$1/2$ pint	=	$1/4$ litre
scant 1 pint	=	$1/2$ litre
$1^3/4$ pints	=	1 litre
1 gallon	=	4.5 litres

Liquid Measures

1 pint	=	20 fl oz	=	32 tablespoons
$1/2$ pint	=	10 fl oz	=	16 tablespoons
$1/4$ pint	=	5 fl oz	=	8 tablespoons
$1/8$ pint	=	$2^1/2$ fl oz	=	4 tablespoons
$1/16$ pint	=	$1^1/4$ fl oz	=	2 tablespoons

Solid Measures

1 oz almonds, ground = $3^3/4$ level tablespoons
1 oz breadcrumbs fresh = 7 level tablespoons
1 oz butter, lard = 2 level tablespoons
1 oz cheese, grated = $3^1/2$ level tablespoons
1 oz cocoa = $2^3/4$ level tablespoons
1 oz desiccated coconut = $4^1/2$ tablespoons
1 oz cornflour = $2^1/2$ tablespoons
1 oz custard powder = $2^1/2$ tablespoons
1 oz curry powder and spices = 5 tablespoons
1 oz flour = 2 level tablespoons
1 oz rice, uncooked = $1^1/2$ tablespoons
1 oz sugar, caster and granulated = 2 tablespoons
1 oz icing sugar = $2^1/2$ tablespoons
1 oz yeast, granulated = 1 level tablespoon

American Measures

16 fl oz	=1 American pint
8 fl oz	=1 American standard cup
0.50 fl oz	=1 American tablespoon

(slightly smaller than British Standards Institute tablespoon)

0.16 fl oz	=1 American teaspoon

Australian Cup Measures
(Using the 8-liquid-ounce cup measure)

1 cup flour	4 oz
1 cup sugar (crystal or caster)	8 oz
1 cup icing sugar (free from lumps)	5 oz
1 cup shortening (butter, margarine)	8 oz
1 cup brown sugar (lightly packed)	4 oz
1 cup soft breadcrumbs	2 oz
1 cup dry breadcrumbs	3 oz
1 cup rice (uncooked)	6 oz
1 cup rice (cooked)	5 oz
1 cup mixed fruit	4 oz
1 cup grated cheese	4 oz
1 cup nuts (chopped)	4 oz
1 cup coconut	$2^1/2$ oz

Australian Spoon Measures

	level tablespoon
1 oz flour	2
1 oz sugar	$1^1/2$
1 oz icing sugar	2
1 oz shortening	1
1 oz honey	1
1 oz gelatine	2
1 oz cocoa	3
1 oz cornflour	$2^1/2$
1 oz custard powder	$2^1/2$

Australian Liquid Measures
(Using 8-liquid-ounce cup)

1 cup liquid	8 oz
$2^1/2$ cups liquid	20 oz (1 pint)
2 tablespoons liquid	1 oz
1 gill liquid	5 oz ($1/4$ pint)